Borders, Dumfries & Galloway

Alan Murphy

D1348042

Credits

Footprint credits
Editor: Stephanie Rebello
Production and layout: Emma Bryers
Maps: Kevin Feeney
Cover: Pepi Bluck

Publisher: Patrick Dawson
Managing Editor: Felicity Laughton
Advertising: Elizabeth Taylor
Sales and marketing: Kirsty Holmes

Photography credits
Front cover: Dennis Dolkens/
Dreamstime.com
Back cover: Creative Nature Media/
Shutterstock.com

Printed in Great Britain by CPI Antony Rowe,
Chippenham, Wiltshire

MIX
Paper from
responsible sources
FSC® C013604
www.fsc.org

Every effort has been made to ensure that
the facts in this guidebook are accurate.
However, travellers should still obtain advice
from consulates, airlines, etc, about travel
and visa requirements before travelling.
The authors and publishers cannot accept
responsibility for any loss, injury or
inconvenience however caused.

Contains Ordnance Survey data
© Crown copyright and database
right 2013

Publishing information
Footprint *Focus Borders, Dumfries & Galloway*
1st edition
© Footprint Handbooks Ltd
March 2013

ISBN: 978 1 909268 25 8
CIP DATA: A catalogue record for this book
is available from the British Library

® Footprint Handbooks and the Footprint
mark are a registered trademark of
Footprint Handbooks Ltd

Published by Footprint
6 Riverside Court
Lower Bristol Road
Bath BA2 3DZ, UK
T +44 (0)1225 469141
F +44 (0)1225 469461
footprinttravelguides.com

Distributed in the USA by Globe Pequot
Press, Guilford, Connecticut

The content of Footprint *Focus Borders,
Dumfries & Galloway* has been taken directly
from Footprint's *Scotland Handbook* which
was researched and written by Alan Murphy.

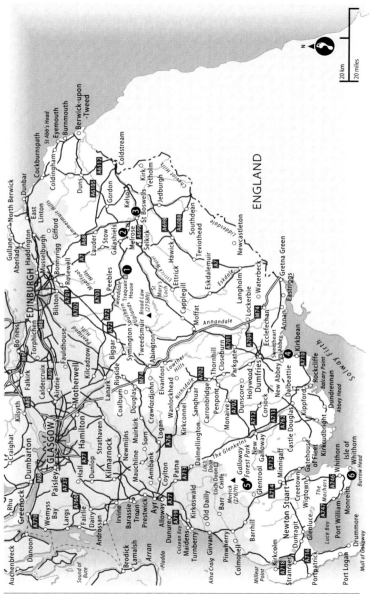

The vast swathe of Southern Scotland covered in this guide is an area usually overlooked by those on their way to Glasgow, Edinburgh or further north. Consequently, it is relatively free from the litterstrewn lay-bys and crowded beauty spots of more favoured parts.

Southern Scotland is divided neatly by the A74(M), the main route from England to Scotland. To the east of this line the main tourist focus is the Borders region, with its peaceful little mill towns, in particular lovely little Melrose. To the north are the narrow ranges of the Lammermuir, Moorfoot and Pentland Hills.

The landscape becomes ever more wild and mountainous as you head west from the Tweed Valley across the Southern Uplands. Some of the area's most spectacular scenery is west of Dumfries, in the Galloway Forest Park. The Solway Coast, from Dumfries to the Mull of Galloway, is equally appealing.

Despite its proximity to the English border, the south of Scotland is in many ways at the very heart of the country. Under constant threat during the long wars with England, its people were at the front line in the defence of Scottish nationhood. It is therefore no coincidence that one of Scotland's greatest literary figures, Sir Walter Scott, was born and lived here.

Planning your trip

Best time to visit the Borders, Dumfries and Galloway

The only predictable thing about the weather in Scotland is its unpredictability. You can have blazing sunshine in April, pouring rain in July and a blizzard in May. So, you'll need to be prepared for everything. Climbers and walkers especially must take heed of all weather warnings. It can be hot enough for bikinis in the car park at the foot of a 2000-ft mountain, and two hours later near the summit you're faced with driving, horizontal hail, rain or snow and unable to see further than the end of your nose.

The midge is the scourge of many a Highland holiday: a ferocious, persistent and unbelievably irritating little beast that thrives in damp, humid conditions and will drive you to the edge of sanity. For details on how best to combat this little terror, see page 21.

Getting to the Borders, Dumfries and Galloway

Air
Generally speaking, the cheapest and quickest way to travel to Scotland from outside the UK is by air. There are good links to Edinburgh and Glasgow, with direct flights from many European cities, and direct flights from North America to Glasgow. There are also flights from a few European cities to Aberdeen and Inverness. There are no direct flights from North America to Edinburgh; these are usually routed via London or Dublin. There are also daily flights from Ireland and regular flights to most Scottish airports from other parts of the UK. There are no direct flights to Scotland from Australia, New Zealand, South Africa or Japan; you will have to get a connection from London.

From the UK and Ireland There are direct flights to Scotland's four main airports – Glasgow, Edinburgh, Aberdeen and Inverness – almost hourly from London Heathrow, Gatwick, Stansted and Luton airports. There are also daily flights from provincial UK airports and from Dublin. To fly on to the smaller airports, you'll need to change planes. The cheapest flights leave from London Luton or Stansted, plus a few provincial airports, with **Ryanair** and **easyJet**. If you book online, fares can be as little as £5 one-way during promotions (excluding taxes), but usually you can expect to fly for under £70 return if you can be flexible with dates and times. These tickets are often subject to rigid restrictions, but the savings can make the extra effort worthwhile. Cheaper tickets usually have to be bought at least a week in advance and apply to only a few midweek flights. They are also non-refundable, or only partly refundable, and non-transferable. A standard flexible and refundable fare from London to Glasgow or Edinburgh will cost at least £150-200 return. The flight from London to Glasgow and Edinburgh is roughly one hour.

From the rest of Europe There are direct flights to **Glasgow International** from many European capitals, including Copenhagen, Amsterdam, Paris (Beauvais), Dublin, Frankfurt, Stockholm, Brussels, Milan, Oslo and Barcelona. There are flights to **Edinburgh** from Paris (CDG), Zurich, Amsterdam, Brussels, Copenhagen and Frankfurt; direct flights to **Aberdeen** from Amsterdam, Copenhagen and Stavanger; and to **Inverness** from Amsterdam and Zurich.

Don't miss...

From North America Because of the much larger number of flights to London, it is generally cheaper to fly there first and get an onward flight, see above for the best deals. For low season Apex fares, expect to pay around US$500-700 from New York and other East Coast cities, and around US$700-900 from the West Coast. Prices rise to around US$700-1000 from New York, and up to US$1000 from the West Coast in the summer months. Low season Apex fares from Toronto and Montreal cost around CAN$700-900, and from Vancouver around CAN$800-900, rising during the summer. East Coast USA to Glasgow takes around six to seven hours direct. To London it takes seven hours. From the West Coast it takes an additional four hours.

To Glasgow International Continental Airlines and **KLM** fly from New York, **Aer Lingus** and **KLM** fly from Chicago, and **Air Canada** from Toronto.

Airport information Glasgow International ① *8 miles west of the city, at junction 28 on the M8, T0844-481 5555,* handles domestic and international flights. Terminal facilities include car hire, bank ATMs, currency exchange, left luggage, tourist information (T0141-848 4440), and shops, restaurants and bars. For all public transport information T0871-200 2233. **Edinburgh Airport** ① *T0844-4812 8989 for general enquiries,* has all facilities, including a tourist information desk, currency exchange, ATMs, restaurants and bars (first floor), shops (ground floor and first floor) and car hire desks in the terminal in the main UK arrivals area.

Rail

There are fast and frequent rail services from London and other main towns and cities in England to Glasgow and Edinburgh. Journey time from London is about 4½ hours to Edinburgh, five hours to Glasgow. Two companies operate direct services from London to Scotland: **National Express** trains leave from King's Cross and run up the east coast to Edinburgh and **Virgin** trains leave from Euston and run up the west coast to Glasgow. **ScotRail** operates the *Caledonian Sleeper* service if you wish to travel overnight from London Euston to Edinburgh and Glasgow. This runs nightly from Sunday to Friday. Fares start from £59 per person. For more information, see www.scotrail.co.uk or the excellent www.seat61.com.

 Eurostar ① *T08705-186186 (+44-123-361 7575), www.eurostar.com,* operates high-speed trains through the Channel Tunnel to London St Pancras International from Paris (2½ hours), Brussels (two hours) and Lille (1½ hours). You then have to change trains, and stations, for the onward journey north to Scotland. If you're driving from continental

Europe you could take *Le Shuttle*, which runs 24 hours a day, 365 days a year, and takes you and your car from Calais to Folkestone in 35 to 45 minutes. Standard return fares on *Le Shuttle* range from £98 per car load. Depending on how far in advance you book, or when you travel, cheaper fares are available, call T08705-353535 for bookings.

Enquiries and booking National Rail Enquiries ⓘ *T08457-484950, www.nationalrail.co.uk*, are quick and courteous with information on rail services and fares but not always accurate, so double check. They can't book tickets but will provide you with the relevant telephone number. The website www.qjump.co.uk is a bit hit-and-miss but generally fast and efficient, and shows you all the various options on any selected journey, while www.thetrainline. co.uk also has its idiosyncrasies but shows prices clearly. For advance card bookings, contact **National Express**, T08457-484950, www.nationalexpresseastcoast.com; **ScotRail**, T08457-550033, www.scotrail.co.uk; and **Virgin**, T08457-222333, www.virgintrains.co.uk.

Fares To describe the system of rail ticket pricing as complicated is a huge understatement and impossible to explain here. There are many and various discounted fares, but restrictions are often prohibitive, which explains the long queues and delays at ticket counters in railway stations. The cheapest ticket is an Advance ticket or Value Advance (**Virgin**), which must be booked in advance (obviously), though this is not available on all journeys. A **GNER** London–Edinburgh Advance Single costs between £14-100. Advance Singles with **ScotRail** on this route start from £39.50 for direct trains. All discount tickets should be booked as quickly as possible as they are often sold out weeks, or even months, in advance. A *Caledonian Sleeper* 'Bargain Berth' single ticket from London to Edinburgh or Glasgow costs from £19; to book visit www.travelpass.buytickets.scotrail.co.uk.

Railcards There are a variety of railcards which give discounts on fares for certain groups. Cards are valid for one year and most are available from main stations. You need two passport photos and proof of age or status.

   Young Person's Railcard ⓘ *www.16-25railcard.co.uk*. For those aged 16-25 or full-time students aged 26+ in the UK. Costs £26 for one year and gives 33% discount on most train tickets and some other services.

   Senior Citizen's Railcard ⓘ *www.senior-railcard.co.uk*. For those aged over 60. Same price and discounts as above.

   Disabled Person's Railcard ⓘ *Disabled Person's Railcard Office, PO Box 163, Newcastle-upon-Tyne, NE12 8WX, www.disabledpersons-railcard.co.uk*. Costs £18 and gives 33% discount to a disabled person and one other. Pick up an application form from stations. It may take up to 21 days to process, so apply in advance.

   Family Railcard: Costs £26 and gives 33% discount on most tickets for up to four adults travelling together, and 60% discount for up to four children.

Road
Bus/coach Road links to Scotland are excellent, and a number of companies offer express coach services day and night. This is the cheapest form of travel to Scotland. The main operator between England and Scotland is **National Express** ⓘ *T08717-818178, www. nationalexpress.com*. There are direct buses from most British cities to Edinburgh, Glasgow, Aberdeen and Inverness. Tickets can be bought at bus stations or from a huge number of agents throughout the country. Fares from London to Glasgow and Edinburgh with **National Express** start at around £25 return for a Funfare return (online discount fare).

Fares to Aberdeen and Inverness are a little higher. The London to Glasgow/Edinburgh journey takes around eight hours. From Manchester to Glasgow takes around 6½ hours.

Sea **P&O Irish Sea** ⓘ *T0871-664 2020, www.poferries.com*, has several crossings daily from Larne to Cairnryan (one hour), and from Larne to Troon (two hours). Fares are from £79 each way for for car and driver. **Stena Line** ⓘ *T0870-570 7070, www.stenaline.co.uk*, runs numerous ferries (three hours) and high-speed catamarans (1½ hours) from Belfast to Stranraer, fares from £79 single for car and driver.

Transport in the Borders, Dumfries and Galloway

Exploring the Borders and Dumfries and Galloway is undeniably easier if you have your own transport, though the main tourist centres are easily accessed by bus or train. Getting off the beaten track requires patience but is worthwhile and easily achieved with a little forward planning. An excellent online sources of travel information, including timetables and operators is www.travelinescotland.com. Tourist offices throughout the Borders and Dumfries and Galloway also carry leaflets on their local and regional transport network.

Public transport can also be expensive, though there's a whole raft of discount passes and tickets which can save you a lot of money. Hiring a car can work out as a more economical, and certainly more flexible, option, especially for more than two people travelling together. It will also enable you to get off the beaten track and see more of the country.

Rail
The rail network in Scotland is limited and train travel is comparatively expensive, but trains are a fast and effective way to get around and also provide some beautifully scenic journeys.

ScotRail operates most train services within Scotland. You can buy train tickets at the stations, from major travel agents, or over the phone with a credit or debit card. For information and advance credit or debit card bookings visit www.scotrail.co.uk. Details of services are given throughout the guide. For busy long-distance routes it's best to reserve a seat. Seat reservations to Edinburgh, Glasgow, Aberdeen or Inverness are included in the price of the ticket when you book in advance. If the ticket office is closed, there's usually a machine on the platform. If this isn't working, you can buy a ticket on the train. Cyclists should note that though train companies have a more relaxed attitude to taking bikes on trains, reservations at a small fee for bikes are still required on some services. Cycles are carried free of charge on **ScotRail** services, although reservations are required on longer distance routes.

Eurorail passes are not recognized in Britain, but **ScotRail** offers a couple of worthwhile travel passes. The most flexible is the **Freedom of Scotland Travelpass**, which gives unlimited rail travel within Scotland. The Central Scotland Rover allows unlimited travel in the central belt of Scotland from the East Coast, Edinburgh, Stirling and Fife to Glasgow, and also covers unlimited travel on the Glasgow Underground network.

Road
Bus and coach Travelling around Scotland by bus takes longer than the train but is much cheaper. There are numerous local bus companies, but the main operator is **Scottish Citylink** ⓘ *T08705-505050, www.citylink.co.uk*. Bus services between towns and cities are good, but far less frequent in more remote rural areas. Note that long-distance express buses are called coaches. There are a number of discount and flexible tickets available and details of these are given on the **Citylink** website, which is fast and easy to use.

Walks and trails

The south of Scotland is excellent walking country, and there are numerous marked trails through the forests and hills and circular walks around the towns, especially in the Tweed Valley. The tourist offices have leaflets detailing all the main routes. There are also a number of Ranger-led walks, details of which are also available at tourist offices. For the more ambitious hiker there are two long-distance trails. The 62-mile St Cuthbert's Way, see page 34, a cross-border trail, and the most famous and demanding of walks, the 212-mile Southern Upland Way, see page 71.

Available to overseas passport holders, the **Brit Xplorer Pass** offers unlimited travel on all **National Express** buses. They can be bought from major airports and bus terminals. **Scottish Citylink** runs a daily bus service between Scotland's six cities and strategic ports. It offers a diverse range of discount and saver cards including an Explorer Pass that offers unlimited travel on its routes for a specified number of days.

Car and campervan Travelling with your own private transport is the ideal way to explore the country. This allows you to cover a lot of ground in a short space of time and to reach remote places. The main disadvantages are rising fuel costs (around £1.50 per litre for diesel), traffic congestion and parking, but the latter two are only a problem in the main cities and on the motorways in the Central Belt.

To drive in Scotland you must have a current **driving licence**. Foreign nationals also need an international **driving permit**, available from state and national motoring organizations for a small fee. Those importing their own vehicle should also have their vehicle registration or ownership document. Make sure you're adequately **insured**. In all of the UK you drive on the left. **Speed limits** are 30 miles per hour (mph) in built-up areas, 70 mph on motorways and dual carriageways, and 60 mph on most other roads.

It's advisable to join one of the main UK motoring organizations during your visit for their 24-hour breakdown assistance. The two main ones in Britain are the **Automobile Association** (**AA**) ⓘ *T0800-085 2721, www.theaa.com*, and the **Royal Automobile Club** (**RAC**) ⓘ *T08705-722722, www.rac.co.uk*. One year's membership of the AA starts at £30 and £28 for the RAC. They also provide many other services, including a reciprocal agreement for free assistance with many overseas motoring organizations. Check to see if your organization is included. Both companies can also extend their cover to include Europe. Their emergency numbers are: **AA**, T0800-887766; **RAC**, T0800-828282. You can call these numbers even if you're not a member, but you'll have to a pay a large fee. In remote areas you may have to wait a long time for assistance.

Car hire need not be expensive in Scotland if you shop around for the best deals. **AVIS** offers weekend rates from around £45 and £126 for the week, though whichever operator you choose be wary of high charges for additional mileage. Even without deals you should be able to hire a small car for a week from £150. Local hire companies often offer better deals than the larger multi-nationals, though **easyCar** can offer the best rates, at around £10 per day, if you book in advance and don't push up the charges with high mileage. They are based at Aberdeen, Glasgow, Edinburgh and Inverness airport. Many companies such as **Europcar** offer the flexibility of picking up in Glasgow and leaving in Edinburgh, and vice versa. Most companies prefer payment with a credit card, otherwise you'll have to leave a large deposit (£100 or more). You'll need a full driver's licence (one or two years) and be aged over 21 (23 in some cases).

Alternatively, why not hire your own transport and accommodation at the same time by renting a campervan. Campervans can be rented from a number of companies and it's best to arrange this before arriving as everything gets booked up in the high season (June to August).

Hitching As in the rest of the UK, hitching is never entirely safe, and is certainly not advised for anyone travelling alone, particularly women travellers. Those prepared to take the risk may get a lift but you will probably have to wait a while even to see a vehicle in remoter parts.

Where to stay in the Borders, Dumfries and Galloway

Staying in the region can mean anything from being pampered to within an inch of your life in a baronial mansion to roughing it in a basic youth hostel. If you have the money, then the sky is very much the limit in terms of sheer splendour and excess. We have listed many of the top class establishments in this book, with a bias towards those that offer that little bit extra in terms of character. Those spending less may have to forego the four-posters and Egyptian cotton sheets but there are still many good-value small hotels and guesthouses with that essential wow factor – especially when it comes to the views. At the bottom end of the scale, there are also some excellent hostels in some pretty special locations.

We have tried to give as broad a selection as possible to cater for all tastes and budgets but if you can't find what you're after, or if someone else has beaten you to the draw, then the tourist information centres (TICs) will help find accommodation for you. They can recommend a place within your particular budget and give you the number to phone up and book yourself, or will book a room for you. Some offices charge a small fee (usually £1) for booking a room, while others ask you to pay a deposit of 10% which is deducted from your first night's bill. Details of town and city TICs are given throughout the guide. There are also several websites that you can browse and book accommodation. Try www.visitscotland.com, www.scottishaccommodationindex.com, www.aboutscotland.com, www.scotland2000.com and www.assc.co.uk.

Accommodation in Scotland will be your greatest expense, particularly if you are travelling on your own. Single rooms are in short supply and many places are reluctant to let a double room to one person, even when they're not busy. Single rooms are usually more than the cost per person for a double room and in some cases cost the same as two people sharing a double room.

Hotels, guesthouses and B&Bs

Area tourist boards publish accommodation lists that include campsites, hostels, self-catering accommodation and VisitScotland-approved hotels, guesthouses and bed and breakfasts (B&Bs). Places participating in the **VisitScotland** system will have a plaque displayed outside which shows their grading, determined by a number of stars ranging from one to five. These reflect the level of facilities, as well as the quality of hospitality and service. However, do not assume that a B&B, guesthouse or hotel is no good because it is not listed by the tourist board. They simply don't want to pay to be included in the system, and some of them may offer better value. If you'd like to stay in a Scottish castle as a paying guest of the owner, contact **Scotts Castle Holidays** ⓘ *T01208-821341, www.scottscastles.com*.

Hotels At the top end of the scale there are some fabulously luxurious hotels, often in spectacular locations. Many of them are converted baronial mansions or castles, and offer a chance to enjoy a taste of aristocratic grandeur and style. At the lower end of the scale, there is often little to choose between cheaper hotels and guesthouses or B&Bs. The latter often offer higher standards of comfort and a more personal service, but many smaller hotels are really just guesthouses, and are often family-run and every bit as friendly. Note that some hotels, especially in town centres or in fishing ports, may also be rather noisy, as the bar can often be the social hub. Rooms in most mid-range to expensive hotels almost always have bathrooms en suite. Many upmarket hotels offer excellent room-only deals in the low season. An efficient last-minute hotel booking service is www.laterooms.com,

Price codes

Where to stay

££££ £160 and over	**£££** £90-160
££ £50-90	**£** under £50

Prices quoted are for a double room in high season.

Restaurants

£££ over £30	**££** £15-30	**£** under £15

Prices quoted are for a two-course meal excluding drink or service charge.

which specializes in weekend breaks. Also note that many hotels offer cheaper rates for online booking through agencies such as www.lastminute.com.

Guesthouses Guesthouses are often large, converted family homes with up to five or six rooms. They tend to be slightly more expensive than B&Bs, charging between £30 and £50 per person per night, and though they are often less personal, usually provide better facilities, such as en suite bathroom, colour TV in each room and private parking. In many instances they are more like small budget hotels. Many guesthouses offer evening meals, though this may have to be requested in advance.

Bed and breakfasts (B&Bs) B&Bs provide the cheapest private accommodation. At the bottom end of the scale you can get a bedroom in a private house, a shared bathroom and a huge cooked breakfast for around £20-25 per person per night. Small B&Bs may only have one or two rooms to let, so it's important to book in advance during the summer season and in the remoter parts where accommodation options are more limited. More upmarket B&Bs have en suite bathrooms and TVs in each room and usually charge from £25-35 per person per night. In general, B&Bs are more hospitable, informal, friendlier and offer better value than hotels. Many B&B owners are also a great source of local knowledge and can even provide OS maps for local walks. B&Bs in the Outer Hebrides and other remote locations also offer dinner, bed and breakfast, which is useful as eating options are limited, especially on a Sunday.

Some places, especially in ferry ports, charge room-only rates, which are slightly cheaper and allow you to get up in time to catch an early morning ferry. However, this means that you miss out on a huge cooked breakfast. If you're travelling on a tight budget, you can eat as much as you can at breakfast time and save on lunch as you won't need to eat again until evening. This is particularly useful if you're heading into the hills, as you won't have to carry so much food. Many B&B owners will even make up a packed lunch for you at a small extra cost.

Hostels

For those travelling on a tight budget, there is a large network of hostels offering cheap accommodation. These are also popular centres for backpackers and provide a great opportunity for meeting fellow travellers. Hostels have kitchen facilities for self-catering, and some include a continental breakfast in the price or provide cheap breakfasts and evening meals. Advance booking is recommended at all times, particularly from May to September and on public holidays, and a credit card is often useful.

Pitch a tent on the wild side

The Land Reform (Scotland) Act 2003, which together with the Scottish Access Code came into effect in February 2005, ensures Scotland offers walkers, canoeists, cyclists and campers some of the most liberal land access laws in Europe. Technically it means you have the 'right to roam' almost anywhere, although the emphasis is on 'responsible access' (see www.outdooraccess-scotland.com).

Scottish Youth Hostel Association (SYHA) The **Scottish Youth Hostel Association (SYHA)** ① *7 Glebe Cres, Stirling, T01786-891400, www.syha.org.uk*, is separate from the YHA in England and Wales. It has a network of over 60 hostels, which are often better and cheaper than those in other countries. They offer bunk-bed accommodation in single-sex dormitories or smaller rooms, kitchen and laundry facilities. The average cost is £10-20 per person per night. Though some rural hostels are still strict on discipline and impose a 2300 curfew, those in larger towns and cities tend to be more relaxed and doors are closed as late as 0200. Some larger hostels provide breakfasts for around £2.50 and three-course evening meals for £4-5. For all EU residents, adult membership costs £10, and can be obtained at the SYHA National Office, or at the first SYHA hostel you stay at. SYHA membership gives automatic membership of **Hostelling International** (**HI**). The SYHA produces a handbook (free with membership) giving details of all their youth hostels, including transport links. This can be useful as some hostels are difficult to get to without your own transport. You should always phone ahead, as many hostels are closed during the day and phone numbers are listed in this guide. Many hostels are closed during the winter, details are given in the SYHA Handbook. Youth hostel members are entitled to various discounts, including 20% off Edinburgh bus tours, 20% off Scottish Citylink tickets and 33% off the Orkney Bus (Inverness–Kirkwall).

Independent hostels Details of most independent hostels (or 'bunkhouses') can be found in the annual Independent Hostel Guide, www.independenthostelguide.com. The **Independent Backpackers Hostels of Scotland** is an association of nearly 100 independent hostels/bunkhouses throughout Scotland. This association has a programme of inspection and lists members in their free '*Blue Guide*'. Independent hostels tend to be more laid-back, with fewer rules and no curfew, and no membership is required. They all have dormitories, hot showers and self-catering kitchens. Some include continental breakfast or provide cheap breakfasts. All these hostels are listed on their excellent website, www.hostel-scotland.co.uk.

Campsites and self-catering

Campsites There are hundreds of campsites around Scotland. They are mostly geared to caravans, and vary greatly in quality and level of facilities. The most expensive sites, which charge up to £15 to pitch a tent, are usually well equipped. Sites are usually only open from April to October. If you plan to do a lot of camping, you should check out www.scottish camping.com, which is the most comprehensive service with over 500 sites, many with pictures and reviews from punters. North Americans planning on camping should invest in an international camping carnet, which is available from home motoring organizations, or from **Family Campers and RVers** (**FCRV**) ① *4804 Transit Rd, Building 2, Depew, NY 14043, T1-800-245 9755, www.fcrv.org*. It gives you discounts at member sites.

Self-catering There are lots of different types of accommodation to choose from, to suit all budgets, ranging from luxury lodges, castles and lighthouses to wooden cabins with no electricity. The minimum stay is usually one week in the summer peak season, though many offer shorter stays of two, three or four nights, especially outside the peak season. Expect to pay at least £200-400 per week for a two-bedroom cottage in the winter, rising to £400-1000 in the high season, or more if it's a particularly nice place. A good source of self-catering accommodation is the VisitScotland's guide, which lists over 1200 properties and is available to buy from any tourist office, but there are also dozens of excellent websites to browse. Amongst the best websites are the following: www.cottages-and-castles.co.uk; www.scottish-country-cottages.co.uk; www.cottages4you.co.uk; www.rural retreats.co.uk; and www.assc.co.uk. If you want to tickle a trout or feed a pet lamb check out www.farmstay.co.uk, which offers over a thousand good value rural places to stay around the UK, all clearly listed on a clickable map.

The **National Trust for Scotland** ① *28 Charlotte Sq, Edinburgh, T0844-493 2100, www. nts.org.uk*, owns many historic properties which are available for self-catering holidays, sleeping between two and 15 people. Prices start at around £300 per week in high season rising to £1000 for the top of the range lodges.

Food and drink in the Borders, Dumfries and Galloway

While Scotland's national drink is loved the world over, Scottish cooking hasn't exactly had good press over the years. This is perhaps not too surprising, as the national dish, haggis, consists of a stomach stuffed with diced innards and served with mashed tatties (potatoes) and *neeps* (turnips). Not a great start. And things got even worse when the Scots discovered the notorious deep-fried Mars bar.

However, Scottish cuisine has undergone a dramatic transformation in the last decade and Scotland now boasts some of the most talented chefs, creating some of the best food in Britain. The heart of Scottish cooking is local produce, which includes the finest fish, shellfish, game, lamb, beef and vegetables, and a vast selection of traditionally made cheeses. What makes Scottish cooking so special is ready access to these foods. What could be better than enjoying an aperitif whilst watching your dinner being delivered by a local fisherman, knowing that an hour later you'll be enjoying the most delicious seafood?

Modern Scottish cuisine is now a feature of many of the top restaurants in the country. This generally means the use of local ingredients with foreign-influenced culinary styles, in particular French. International cuisine is also now a major feature on menus all over the country, influenced by the rise of Indian and Chinese restaurants in recent decades. In fact, so prevalent are exotic Asian and Oriental flavours that curry has now replaced fish and chips (fish supper) as the nation's favourite food.

Food

Fish, meat and game form the base of many of the country's finest dishes. Scottish beef, particularly Aberdeen Angus, is the most famous in the world. This will, or should, usually be hung for at least four weeks and sliced thick. Game is also a regular feature of Scottish menus, though it can be expensive, especially venison (deer), but delicious and low in cholesterol. Pheasant and hare are also tasty, but grouse is, quite frankly, overrated.

Fish and seafood are fresh and plentiful, and if you're travelling around the northwest coast you must not miss the chance to savour local mussels, prawns, oysters, scallops, langoustines, lobster or crab. Salmon is, of course, the most famous of Scottish fish, but you're more likely to be served the fish-farmed variety than 'wild' salmon, which has a more delicate flavour. Trout is also farmed extensively, but the standard of both remains high. Kippers are also a favourite delicacy, the best of which come from Loch Fyne or the Achiltibuie smokery. Proper fish and chips in Scotland are made with haddock; cod is for Sassenachs (the English) and cats.

Haggis has made something of a comeback, and small portions are often served as starters in fashionable restaurants. Haggis is traditionally eaten on Burns Night (25 January) in celebration of the great poet's birthday, when it is piped to the table and then slashed open with a sword at the end of a recital of Robert Burns' *Address to the Haggis*. Other national favourites feature names to relish: **cock-a-leekie** is a soup made from chicken, leeks and prunes; **cullen skink** is a delicious concoction of smoked haddock and potatoes; while at the other end of the scale of appeal is **hugga-muggie**, a Shetland dish using fish's stomach. There's also the delightfully named **crappit heids** (haddock heads stuffed with lobster) and **partan bree** (a soup made form giant crab's claws, cooked with rice). Rather more mundane is the ubiquitous **Scotch broth**, made with mutton stock, vegetables, barley, lentils and split peas, and **stovies**, which is a hearty mash of potato, onion and minced beef.

Waist-expanding puddings or desserts are a very important part of Scottish cooking and often smothered in butterscotch sauce or syrup. There is a huge variety, including **cranachan**, a mouth-watering mix of toasted oatmeal steeped in whisky, cream and fresh raspberries, and **Atholl brose**, a similar confection of oatmeal, whisky and cream.

Eaten before pudding, in the French style, or afterwards, are Scotland's many home-produced cheeses, which have made a successful comeback in the face of mass-produced varieties. Many of the finest cheeses are produced on the islands, especially Arran, Mull, Islay and Orkney. **Caboc** is a creamy soft cheese rolled in oatmeal and is made in the Highlands.

Anyone staying at a hotel, guesthouse or B&B will experience the hearty **Scottish breakfast**, which includes bacon, egg, sausage, 'tattie scone' and black pudding (a type of sausage made with blood), all washed down with copious quantities of tea. Coffee is readily available everywhere, with most places now offering a selection of cappuccinos and café lattes. You may also be served kippers (smoked herring) or porridge, an erstwhile Scottish staple. Made with oatmeal and with the consistency of Italian polenta, it is traditionally eaten with salt, though heretics are offered sugar instead. Oatcakes (oatmeal biscuits) may also be on offer, as well as potato scones, baps (bread rolls) or bannocks (a sort of large oatcake). After such a huge cooked breakfast you probably won't feel like eating again until dinner.

Drink

Beer Beer is the alcoholic drink of choice in Scotland. The most popular type of beer is lager, which is generally brewed in the UK, even when it bears the name of an overseas brand, and is almost always weaker in both strength and character than the lagers in mainland Europe. However, examples of the older and usually darker type of beers, known as ales, are still widely available, and connoisseurs should try some of these as they are far more rewarding. Indeed, the best of them rival Scotland's whiskies as gourmet treats.

Traditionally, Scottish ales were graded by the shilling, an old unit of currency written as /-, according to strength. This system is still widely used by the older established breweries, though many of the newer independents and 'micros' have departed from it. 70/- beers at around 3.5% ABV (alcohol by volume), known as 'heavy', and 80/- beers

Turn water into whisky

Malt whisky is made by first soaking dry barley in tanks of local water for two to three days. Then the barley is spread out on a concrete floor or placed in cylindrical drums and allowed to germinate for between eight and 12 days, after which it is dried in a kiln, heated by a peat fire. Next, the dried malt is ground and mixed with hot water in a huge circular vat called a 'mash tun'. A sugary liquid called 'wort' is then drawn from the porridge-like result and piped into huge containers where living yeast is stirred into the mix in order to convert the sugar in the wort into alcohol. After about 48 hours the 'wash' is transferred to copper pot stills and heated till the alcohol vaporizes and is then condensed by a cooling plant into distilled alcohol which is passed through a second still. Once distilled, the liquid is poured into oak casks and left to age for a minimum of three years, though a good malt will stay casked for at least eight years.

(4.5% sometimes known as 'export'), are the most popular, while 60/-, 'light' (3-3.5%) is harder to find. Very strong 90/- beers (6.5% + ABV), known as 'wee heavies', are also brewed, mainly for bottling.

The market is dominated by the giant international brewers: Scottish Courage with its McEwans and Youngers brands; Interbrew with Calders and Carslberg; and Tetley with Tennents lagers. Tennents was the first British brewery to produce a continental-style lager commercially back in the 19th century, and, despite a competitive marketplace, remains a favourite for many Scots.

Much better are the ales from smaller independent breweries. Edinburgh's Caledonian is a world-class brewer producing many excellent beers, including a popular 80/- and a renowned golden hoppy ale, Deuchars IPA. Belhaven, an old, established family brewery in Dunbar, has some superb traditional beers including a malty 80/-, once marketed as the Burgundy of Scotland. Broughton, a microbrewery in the Borders, produces the fruity Greenmantle and an oatmeal stout. Another micro, Harvieston of Clackmannanshire (once an important brewing country), offers a wide and adventurous range of specialities, including Ptarmigan 80/- and a naturally brewed cask lager, Schiehallion. The Heather Ale Company, near Glasgow, has the spicy, unusual Fraoch (pronounced 'Frooch'), which is flavoured with real heather and hops.

Draught beer in pubs and bars is served in pints, or half pints, and you'll pay between £2.50 and £3.50 for a pint (unless you discover a 'Happy Hour' offering good deals on drinks, usually for much more than one hour! Happy hours usually apply in late afternoon or early evening). In many pubs the basic ales are chilled under gas pressure like lagers, but the best ales, such as those from the independents, are 'real ales', still fermenting in the cask and served cool but not chilled (around 12°C) under natural pressure from a handpump, electric pump or air pressure fount. All Scottish beers are traditionally served with a full, creamy head.

Whisky There is no greater pleasure on an inclement evening than enjoying a malt whisky in front of a roaring log fire whilst watching the rain outside pelt down relentlessly. The roots of Scotland's national drink (uisge beatha, or 'water of life' in Gaelic) go back to the late 15th century, but it wasn't until the invention of a patent still in the early 19th century that distilling began to develop from small family-run operations to the large manufacturing business it has become today. Now more than 700 million bottles a year are exported, mainly to the United States, France, Japan and Spain.

There are two types of whisky: single malt, made only from malted barley; and grain, which is made from malted barley together with unmalted barley, maize or other cereals, and is faster and cheaper to produce. Most of the popular brands are blends of both types of whisky – usually 60-70% grain to 30-40% malt. These blended whiskies account for over 90% of all sales worldwide, and most of the production of single malts is used to add flavour to a blended whisky. Amongst the best-known brands of blended whisky are Johnnie Walker, Bells, Teachers and Famous Grouse. There's not much between them in terms of flavour and they are usually drunk with a mixer, such as water or soda.

Single malts are a different matter altogether. Each is distinctive and should be drunk neat to appreciate fully its subtle flavours, though some believe that the addition of water helps free the flavours. Single malts vary enormously. Their distinctive flavours and aromas are derived from the peat used for drying, the water used for mashing, the type of oak cask used and the location of the distillery. Single malts fall into four groups: Highland, Lowland, Campbeltown and Islay. There are over 40 distilleries, most offering guided tours. The majority are located around Speyside, in the northeast. The region's many distilleries include that perennial favourite, Glenfiddich, which is sold in 185 countries. Recommended alternatives are the produce of the beautiful and peaceful Isle of Islay, whose malts are lovingly described in terms of their peaty quality and the produce of the island known as 'Scotland in Miniature', Arran, whose 10-year-old malt, distilled in Lochranza, has won international acclaim. Scots tend to favour the 10-year-old Glenmorangie, while the most popular in the USA is The Macallan.

Eating out

There are places to suit every taste and budget. In the large towns and cities you'll find a vast selection of eating places, including Indian, Chinese, Italian and French restaurants, as well as Thai, Japanese, Mexican, Spanish and, of course, Scottish, but beyond the main cities, choice is much more limited. More and more restaurants are moving away from national culinary boundaries and offering a wide range of international dishes and flavours, so you'll often find Latin American, Oriental and Pacific Rim dishes all on the same menu. This is particularly the case in the many continental-style bistros, brasseries and café-bars, which now offer a more informal alternative to traditional restaurants. Vegetarians are increasingly well catered for in the large cities, where exclusively vegan/vegetarian restaurants and cafés are often the cheapest places to eat, but outside the cities, vegetarian restaurants are thin on the ground, though better-quality eating places will normally offer a reasonable vegetarian selection.

For a cheap meal, your best bet is a pub, hotel bar or café, where you can have a one-course meal for around £5-7 or less, though don't expect gourmet food. The best value is often at lunchtime, when many restaurants offer three-course set lunches or business lunches for less than £10. You'll need a pretty huge appetite to feel like eating a three-course lunch after your gigantic cooked breakfast, however. Also good value are the pre-theatre dinners offered by many restaurants in the larger towns and cities (you don't need to have a theatre ticket to take advantage). These are usually available from around 1730-1800 until 1900-1930, so you could get away with just a sandwich for lunch. At the other end of the price scale are many excellent restaurants where you can enjoy the finest of Scottish cuisine, often with a continental influence, and these are often found in hotels. You can expect to pay from around £30 a head up to £40 or £50 (excluding drinks) in the very top establishments.

The biggest problem with eating out in Scotland, as in the rest of the UK, is the ludicrously limited serving hours in some pubs and hotels, particularly in remoter locations. These places only serve food during restricted hours, seemingly ignorant of the eating habits of foreign visitors, or those who would prefer a bit more flexibility during their holiday. In small places especially, it can be difficult finding food outside these enforced times. Places that serve food all day till 2100 or later are restaurants, fast-food outlets and the many chic bistros and café-bars, which can be found not only in the main cities but increasingly in smaller towns. The latter often offer very good value and above-average quality fare.

Essentials A-Z

Accident and emergency
For police, fire brigade, ambulance and, in certain areas, mountain rescue or coastguard, T999 or T112.

Disabled travellers
For travellers with disabilities, visiting Scotland independently can be a difficult business. While most theatres, cinemas, libraries and modern tourist attractions are accessible to wheelchairs, tours of many historic buildings and finding accommodation remains problematic. Many large, new hotels do have disabled suites, but far too many B&Bs, guesthouses and smaller hotels remain ill-equipped to accept bookings from people with disabilities. However, through the work of organizations like **Disability Scotland** the Government is being pressed to further improve the Disability Discrimination Act and access to public amenities and transport. As a result, many buses and **FirstScotRail**'s train services now accommodate wheelchair-users whilst city taxis should carry wheelchair ramps.

Wheelchair users, and blind or partially sighted people are automatically given 30-50% discount on train fares, and those with other disabilities are eligible for the **Disabled Person's Railcard**, which costs £18 per year and gives a third off most tickets. If you will need assistance at a railway station, call FirstScotRail before travelling on T0800-912 2901. There are no discounts on buses.

If you are disabled you should contact the travel officer of your national support organization. They can provide literature or put you in touch with travel agents specializing in tours for the disabled. **VisitScotland** produces a guide, *Accessible Scotland*, for disabled travellers, and many local tourist offices can provide accessibility details for their area. Alternatively call its national booking hotline on T0845-225 5121. A useful website is www.atlholidays.

com, which specializes in organizing holidays for disabled travellers, recommends hotels with good facilities and can also arrange rental cars and taxis.
Useful organizations include:
Capability Scotland, ASCS, 11 Ellersly Rd, Edinburgh EH12 6HY, T0131-313 5510, or Textphone 0131-346 2529, www.capability-scotland.org.uk.
The Holiday Care Service, T0845-124 9974, www.holidaycare.org.uk, www.tourismfor all.org.uk. Both websites are excellent sources of information about travel and for identifying accessible accommodation in the UK.
The Royal Association for Disability and Rehabilitation (RADAR), Unit 12, City Forum, 250 City Rd, London EC1V 8AF, T020-7250 3222, www.radar.org.uk. A good source of advice and information. It produces an annual *National Key Scheme Guide* for gaining access to over 6000 toilet facilities across the UK (£10.70 including P&P).

Electricity
The current in Britain is 240V AC. Plugs have 3 square pins and adapters are widely available.

Embassies and consulates
The **Foreign Office** website, www.fco.gov.uk, has a directory of all British embassies overseas.

Health
No vaccinations are required for entry into Britain. Citizens of EU countries are entitled to free medical treatment at National Health Service (NHS) hospitals on production of a European Health Insurance Card (EHIC). For details, see the Department of Health website, www.dh.gov.uk/travellers. Also, Australia, New Zealand and several other non-EU European countries have reciprocal healthcare arrangements with Britain. Citizens of other countries will have to pay

Once bitten, twice shy

The major problem facing visitors to many parts of Scotland during the summer months is *Culicoides impunctatus* – or the midge, as it's more commonly known. These tiny flying creatures are savage and merciless in the extreme and hunt in huge packs. Indeed, it is estimated that midges cost the Scottish tourist industry some £286 million in lost revenue. No sooner have you left your B&B for a pleasant evening stroll, than a cloud of these bloodthirsty little devils will descend, getting into your eyes, ears, nose and mouth – and a few places you forgot you even had. The only way to avoid them is to take refuge indoors, or to hide in the nearest loch.

Midges are at their worst in the evening and in damp, shaded or overcast conditions, and between late May and September, but they don't like direct sunlight, heavy rain, smoke and wind. Make sure you're well covered up and wear light-coloured clothing (they're attracted to dark colours). Most effective is a midge net, if you don't mind everyone pointing and laughing at you. Insect repellents have some effect, particularly those with DEET, but those who don't fancy putting chemicals on their skin can try **Mozzy Off** ① *www.mozzy off. com*, which comprises 100% plant oils, while the Thurso-made **Essential Spirit** ① *www.essentialspirit.co.uk*, is also made from natural ingredients. A more radical approach is the Midegeater, a trap which emits carbon dioxide to lure the little blighters within range and then sucks them in at high speed. Those who see prevention as the best form of cure can log on to www.midgeforecast.co.uk, an online midge forecast service that gives five-day predictions of midge movements.

If you do get bitten, spare a thought for the gravedigger from Rùm. According to legend, as punishment for not burying a body properly he was stripped naked, tied to a post and left outside with only the midges for company. The poor chap eventually died of the countless bites.

---

for all medical services, except accident and emergency care given at Accident and Emergency (A&E) Units at most (but not all) National Health Service hospitals. Health insurance is therefore strongly advised for citizens of non-EU countries.

Pharmacists can dispense only a limited range of drugs without a doctor's prescription. Most are open during normal shop hours, though some are open late, especially in larger towns. Local newspapers will carry lists of which are open late. Doctors' surgeries are usually open from around 0830-0900 till 1730-1800, though times vary. Outside surgery hours you can go to the casualty department of the local hospital for any complaint requiring urgent attention. For the address of the nearest hospital or doctors' surgery, www.nhs24.com. See also individual town and city directories throughout the book for details local medical services.

You should encounter no major problems or irritations during your visit to Scotland. The only exceptions are the risk of hyperthermia if you're walking in the mountains in difficult conditions, and the dreaded midge, see box, above.

Money → *US$1 = £0.67, €1 = £0.86 (Mar 2013)*. The British currency is the pound sterling (£), divided into 100 pence (p). Coins come in denominations of 1p, 2p, 5p, 10p, 20p, 50p, £1 and £2. Bank of England banknotes are legal tender in Scotland, in addition to those issued by the Bank of Scotland, Royal Bank of Scotland and Clydesdale Bank. These Scottish banknotes (bills) come in denominations of £5, £10, £20, £50 and

£100 and regardless of what you are told by shopkeepers in England the notes are legal tender in the rest of Britain.

Banks

The larger towns and villages have a branch of at least one of the big 4 high street banks – Bank of Scotland, Royal Bank of Scotland, Clydesdale and TSB Scotland. Bank opening hours are Mon-Fri from 0930 to between 1600 and 1700. Some larger branches may also be open later on Thu and on Sat mornings. In small and remote places, there may be only a mobile bank which runs to a set timetable. This timetable will be available from the local post office.

Banks are usually the best places to change money and cheques. You can withdraw cash from selected banks and ATMs (or cashpoints as they are called in Britain) with your cash and credit card. Though using a debit or credit card is by far the easiest way of keeping in funds, you must check with your bank what the total charges will be; this can be as high as 4-5% in some cases. In more remote parts, ATMs are few and far between and it is important to keep a ready supply of cash on you at all times. Some guesthouses will still request payment in cash. Your bank will give you a list of locations where you can use your card. Bank of Scotland and Royal Bank take Lloyds and Barclays cash cards; Clydesdale takes HSBC and National Westminster cards. Bank of Scotland, Clydesdale and most building society cashpoints are part of the Link network and accept all affiliated cards. See also Credit cards below. In addition to ATMs, bureaux de change can be used outside banking hours. These can be found in most city centres and also at the main airports and train stations. Note that some charge high commissions for changing cheques. Those at international airports, however, often charge less than banks and will change pound sterling cheques for free. Avoid changing money or cheques in hotels, as the rates are usually very poor.

Credit cards

Most hotels, shops and restaurants accept the major credit cards such as MasterCard and Visa and, less frequently, Amex, though some places may charge for using them. They may be less useful in more remote rural areas and smaller establishments such as B&Bs, which will often only accept cash or cheques.

Visa card holders can use the Bank of Scotland, Clydesdale Bank, Royal Bank of Scotland and TSB ATMs; Access/MasterCard holders the Royal Bank and Clydesdale; Amex card holders the Bank of Scotland.

Traveller's cheques

The safest way to carry money is in traveller's cheques. These are available for a small commission from all major banks. American Express (Amex), Visa and Thomas Cook cheques are widely accepted and are the most commonly issued by banks. You'll normally have to pay commission again when you cash each cheque. This will usually be 1%, or a flat rate. No commission is payable on Amex cheques cashed at Amex offices, www.americanexpress.co/feefree. Make sure you keep a record of the cheque numbers and the cheques you've cashed separate from the cheques themselves, so that you can get a full refund of all uncashed cheques should you lose them. It's best to bring sterling cheques to avoid changing currencies twice. Also note that in Britain traveller's cheques are rarely accepted outside banks or foreign exchange bureaux, so you'll need to cash them in advance and keep a good supply of ready cash.

Money transfers

If you need money urgently, the quickest way to have it sent to you is to have it wired to the nearest bank via Western Union, T0800-833833, www.westernunion. co.uk, or Money-gram, T0800-8971 8971. Charges are on a sliding scale; ie it will cost proportionately less to wire out more money. Money can also be wired by Thomas

Cook, www.thomasexchangeglobal.co.uk, or transferred via a bank draft, but this can take up to a week.

Cost of travelling

Scotland can be an expensive place to visit, and prices are higher in more remote parts, but there is plenty of budget accommodation available and backpackers will be able to keep their costs down. Petrol is a major expense and won't just cost an arm and a leg but also the limbs of all remaining family members. Accommodation and restaurant prices also tend to be higher in more popular destinations and during the busy summer months.

The minimum daily budget required, if you're staying in hostels, very cheap B&Bs or camping, cycling or hitching (not recommended), and cooking your own meals, will be around £25-30 per person per day. If you start using public transport and eating out occasionally that will rise to around £35-40. Those staying in slightly more upmarket B&Bs or guesthouses, eating out every evening at pubs or modest restaurants and visiting tourist attractions, such as castles or museums, can expect to pay around £50-60 per day. If you also want to hire a car then costs will rise considerably and you'll be looking at least £75-80 per person per day. Single travellers will have to pay more than ½ the cost of a double room in most places, and should budget on spending around 60-70% of what a couple would spend.

Opening hours

Businesses are usually open Mon-Sat 0900-1700. In towns and cities, as well as villages in holiday areas, many shops open on a Sun but they will open later and close earlier. For TIC opening hours, see page 24.

Post

Most post offices are open Mon-Fri 0900 to 1730 and Sat 0900-1230 or 1300. Smaller sub-post offices are closed for an hour at lunch (1300-1400) and many of them operate out of a shop. Post offices keep the same ½-day closing times as shops.

Stamps can be bought at post offices, but also from vending machines outside, and also at many newsagents. A 1st-class letter weighing up to 100 g to anywhere in the UK costs 60p and should arrive the following day, while 2nd-class letters weighing up to 100 g cost 50p and take between 2-4 days. For more information about Royal Mail postal services, call T08457-740740, or visit www.royalmail.com.

Safety

Incidences of serious crime tend to be the exception rather than the rule and are so rare that they always make front page news. In fact, if someone failed to say 'good morning' – heaven forfend – it would provoke such an outrage that locals would be talking about little else for weeks to come.

Telephone → *Country code +44.*

Useful numbers: operator T100; international operator T155; directory enquiries T192; overseas directory enquiries T153.

Most public payphones are operated by **British Telecom (BT)** and can be found in towns and cities, though less so in rural areas. Numbers of public phone booths have declined in recent years due to the advent of the mobile phone, so don't rely on being able to find a payphone wherever you go. BT payphones take either coins (20p, 50p and £1) or phonecards, which are available at newsagents and post offices displaying the BT logo. These cards come in denominations of £2, £3, £5 and £10. Some payphones also accept credit cards.

For most countries (including Europe, USA and Canada) calls are cheapest Mon-Fri between 1800 and 0800 and all day Sat-Sun. For Australia and New Zealand it's cheapest to call from 1430-1930 and from 2400-0700 every day. Area codes are not needed if calling from within the same area. Any number prefixed by 0800 or 0500 is free to the caller; 08457 numbers are charged at local rates and 08705 numbers at the national rate. To call Scotland from overseas, dial 011 from USA and Canada, 0011 from Australia and 00 from New Zealand, followed by 44, then the area code, minus the first zero, then the number. To call overseas from Scotland dial 00 followed by the country code. Country codes include: Australia 61; Ireland 353; New Zealand 64; South Africa 27; USA and Canada 1.

Time
Greenwich Mean Time (GMT) is used from late Oct to late Mar, after which time the clocks go forward an hour to British Summer Time (BST). GMT is 5 hrs ahead of US Eastern Standard Time and 10 hrs behind Australian Eastern Standard Time.

Tipping
Believe it or not, people in Scotland do leave tips. In a restaurant you should leave a tip of 10-15% if you are satisfied with the service. If the bill already includes a service charge, you needn't add a further tip. Tipping is not normal in pubs or bars. Taxi drivers will expect a tip for longer journeys, usually of around 10%. As in most other countries, porters, bellboys and waiters in more up-market hotels rely on tips to supplement their meagre wages.

Tourist information
The regions covered in this book are served by Scottish Border Tourist Board, www.visitscottishborders.com, and Dumfries and Galloway Tourist Board, www.visitdumfries andgalloway.co.uk, whose tourist offices can provide free information and book local accommodation (for a small fee). From Nov-Mar smaller TIC offices may be closed or have restricted opening hours.

Tourist Information Centres
Tourist offices – called tourist information centres (TICs) – can be found in most Scottish towns. Their addresses, phone numbers and opening hours are listed in the relevant sections of this book. Opening hours vary depending on the time of year, and many of the smaller offices are closed during the winter months. All tourist offices provide information on accommodation, public transport, local attractions and restaurants, as well as selling books, local guides, maps and souvenirs. Many also have free street plans and leaflets describing local walks. They can also book accommodation for you, for a small fee.

Museums, galleries and historic houses
Most of Scotland's tourist attractions, apart from the large museums and art galleries in the main cities, are open only from Easter-Oct. Full details of opening hours and admission charges are given in the relevant sections of this guide.

Over 100 of the country's most prestigious sights, and 75,000 ha of beautiful countryside, are cared for by the **National Trust for Scotland** (NTS), 26-31 Charlotte Sq, Edinburgh EH2 4ET, T0844-493 2100, www.nts.org.uk. National Trust properties are indicated in this guide as 'NTS', and entry charges and opening hours are given for each property.

Historic Scotland (HS), Longmore House, Salisbury Pl, Edinburgh EH9 1SH, T0131-668 8600, www.historic-scotland.gov.uk, manages more than 330 of Scotland's most important castles, monuments and other historic sites. Historic Scotland properties are indicated as 'HS', and admission charges and opening hours are also given in this guide. Historic Scotland offers an **Explorer Pass** which allows free entry to 70 of its properties including Edinburgh and Stirling castles. A 3-day pass (can be used over 5 consecutive days) costs £29, concessions £24, children £17, family £50. A 7-day pass (valid for 14 days) costs £38/£31/£22/£76. It can save a lot of money.

Many other historic buildings are owned by local authorities, and admission is cheap, or in many cases free. Most fee-paying attractions give a discount or concession for senior citizens, the unemployed, full-time students and children under 16 (those under 5 are admitted free everywhere). Proof of age or status must be shown. Many of Scotland's stately homes are still owned and occupied by the landed gentry, and admission is usually between £6 and £12.

Finding out more

The best way of finding out more information for your trip to Scotland is to contact **Visit Scotland** (aka the Scottish Tourist Board), www.visitbritain.com. Alternatively, you can contact **VisitBritain**, the organization that is responsible for tourism throughout the British Isles. Both organizations can provide a wealth of free literature and information such as maps, city guides and accommodation brochures. If particularly interested in ensuring your visit coincides with a major festival or sporting event, it's also worthwhile having a look at **EventScotland**'s website, www. eventscotland.org. Travellers with special needs should also contact Visit Scotland or their nearest VisitBritain office. If you want more detailed information on a particular area, contact the specific tourist boards, see below.

Visas and immigration

Visa regulations are subject to change, so it is essential to check with your local British embassy, high commission or consulate before leaving home. Citizens of all European countries – except Albania, Bosnia Herzegovina, Kosovo, Macedonia, Moldova, Turkey, Serbia and all former Soviet republics (other than the Baltic states) – require only a passport to enter Britain. Citizens of Australia, Canada, New Zealand, South Africa or the USA can stay for up to 6 months, providing they have a return ticket and sufficient funds to cover their stay. Citizens of most other countries require a visa from the commission or consular office in the country of application.

The **Foreign and Commonwealth Office** (FCO), T0207-270 1500, www.fco.gov.uk, has an excellent website, which provides details of British immigration and visa requirements. Also the Home Office UK Border Agency is responsible for UK immigration matters and its website is a good place to start for anyone hoping visit, work, study or emigrate to the UK. Call the immigration enquiry bureau on T0870-606 7766 or visit www.bia.homeoffice.gov.uk.

For visa extensions also contact the **Home Office UK Border Agency** via the above number or its website. The agency can also be reached at Lunar House, Wellesley Rd, Croydon, London CR9. Citizens of Australia, Canada, New Zealand, South Africa or the USA wishing to stay longer than 6 months will need an Entry Clearance Certificate from the British High Commission in their country. For more details, contact your nearest British embassy, consulate or high commission, or the Foreign and Commonwealth Office in London.

Weights and measures

Imperial and metric systems are both in use. Distances on roads are measured in miles and yards, drinks poured in pints and gills, but generally, the metric system is used elsewhere.

Volunteering

See www.volunteerscotland.org.uk.
The British Trust for Conservation Volunteers, Sedum House, Mallard Way, Doncaster DN4 8DB, T01302-388883, www.btcv.org. Get fit in the 'green gym', planting hedges, creating wildlife gardens or improving footpaths.
Earthwatch, 57 Woodstock Rd, Oxford OX2 6HJ, T01865-318838. Team up with scientists studying our furry friends.
Jubilee Sailing Trust, Hazel Rd, Southampton, T023-804 9108, www.jst. org. uk. Work on deck on an adventure holiday.
National Trust for Scotland, Wemyss House, 28 Charlotte Sq, Edinburgh EH2 4ET, T0844-493 2100, www.nts.org.uk. Among a number of Scotland based charities that offer volunteering opportunities.

Contents

Footprint features

Scottish Borders

Scottish Borders

The Scottish Borders cover a huge swathe of southern Scotland to the east of the M74. It's an unspoiled wilderness of green hills, rushing rivers and bleak, barren moors, and it has an austere beauty which would surprise those who think that real Scotland starts somewhere north of Perth. The Borders' proximity to England also gives the region a romantic edge and makes it even more essentially Scottish. This is a part of the country which is drenched in the blood of countless battles with the English, and its many ruined castles and abbeys bear witness to Scotland's long, turbulent relationship with its belligerent southern neighbour. It should come as no surprise, then, that this southern corner of Scotland has so inspired the country's greatest poets and writers. Robert Burns and John Buchan often spoke of its rare charms, but it is Sir Walter Scott, inspired not only by the stark beauty of the countryside but also by its lore and legends, who is most closely associated with the region.

The wildest and most spectacular scenery is to be found in the southern part of the region, along the Yarrow Water, between Selkirk and Moffat, the upper reaches of the Tweed Valley, south of Peebles, and in Liddesdale, southwest of Jedburgh. But it is along the central valley of the River Tweed, between Peebles in the west and Kelso in the east, where you'll find most of the historic attractions, including the fascinating Traquair House, Sir Walter Scott's mansion at Abbotsford. Together with Selkirk, and the textile-producing towns of Galashiels and Hawick, these towns form the heart of the Borders.

Arriving in the Scottish Borders

Getting there and around

There's a good network of buses serving the region's main towns. For all bus information, call the **Borders Council Transport Division** ① *T0300-1001800*. The main operator is **First Edinburgh** ① *T0871-2002233*. There are numerous buses running between the main towns of Galashiels, Melrose, Peebles, Hawick, Selkirk, Jedburgh and Kelso. There are also buses connecting the Border towns with Edinburgh and Berwick-upon-Tweed. There are regular buses from Berwick-upon-Tweed, **Traveline Scotland** ① *www.travelinescotland. com*. **National Express** ① *T08717-818178*, runs services from Newcastle to Edinburgh via Jedburgh, Galashiels and Melrose. The regular bus service is supplemented during the summer months (July to September) by the **Harrier Scenic Bus Services**. Buses make round-trip tours once a week on the following routes: Melrose–Moffat, via Galashiels, Selkirk, Bowhill House, Yarrow, St Mary's Loch (on Thursday); Selkirk–Eyemouth via Galashiels, Melrose, Kelso, Coldstream, Berwick-upon-Tweed; Hawick–Eyemouth via Jedburgh, Town Yetholm, Berwick-upon-Tweed. ▸▸ *For further information, contact the various operators, local TICs and see Transport, page 9.*

The main London–Edinburgh railway line follows the east coast from Berwick-upon-Tweed north to Dunbar in East Lothian. There is no rail link with the Border towns, so you'll have to get off at Berwick and take a bus from there. There's a good road network which allows you to explore the region easily by car. The best way to see the Borders, though, is on foot or by bike. The 90-mile Tweed Cycleway runs past the most important sights, while the Southern Uplands Way takes you through the region's most beautiful and spectacular scenery. ▸▸ *For further details and cycle paths and walks, see page 10.*

Tourist information

There are nine tourist information centres throughout the region. The ones in Jedburgh and Peebles are open all year, and the others (in Coldstream, Eyemouth, Galashiels, Hawick, Kelso, Melrose and Selkirk) are open from April to October. Details are given under each town. Visit www.scot-borders.co.uk.

Peebles and the Tweed Valley → *For listings, see pages 47-52.*

Due south of Edinburgh is the neat and tidy town of Peebles, on the banks of the river Tweed, surrounded by wooded hills. The river here is wide and fast, whereas the pace of life on the town's broad High Street is altogether more sedate. Things liven up somewhat during the week-long Beltane Fair, the great Celtic festival of the sun which is held in June and marks the beginning of summer. Another good time to visit is during the Peebles Arts Festival, which is held over two weeks at the end of August and beginning of September. Peebles is only a 45-minute drive from Edinburgh, and makes a convenient base for a tour of the Tweed Valley.

Peebles and around → *Phone code: 01721. Population: 7000.*

Tweeddale Museum ① *High St, T01721-724820, Apr-Oct Mon-Fri 1000-1200 and 1400-1700, Sat 1000-1200, 1400-1600, winter hours vary, free*, is housed in the Chambers Institute, which was a gift to the town from William Chambers, a native of Peebles and founding publisher of the **Chambers Encyclopaedia**. It houses two notable friezes: one is a copy of the Elgin marbles taken from the Parthenon in Athens (and yet to be returned to their rightful home); the other is the 19th-century Triumph of Alexander. Temporary exhibitions are also staged throughout the year.

Just to the west of town, on the A72, is **Neidpath Castle** (not open to the public), perched high on a rocky bluff overlooking the Tweed. The medieval tower house enjoys an impressive setting. The castle can be reached by following the trail along the River Tweed from Hay Lodge Park in town. The walk passes a beautiful picnic spot beneath the castle and you can swim in the river (but take care). The trail continues through lovely wooded countryside and you can cross the river and return at Manor Bror (a three-mile round trip) or further on at Lyne footbridge (an eight-mile round trip). Details of this and other local walks can be found in the *Popular Walks around Peebles* leaflet available at the tourist office.

Two miles east of town on the A72 is **Glentress Forest**, which has grown over the years to become one of the UK's biggest mountain biking destinations, part of the **7stanes project** ① *www.7stanesmountainbiking.com*, with some of the best singletrack anywhere. There are dozens of tracks through the forest, graded according to level of difficulty. **The Hub in the Forest** ① *T01721-721736, www.thehubintheforest.co.uk*, is an official partner of Forest Enterprise and hires out mountain bikes as well as providing route maps and spares. There's also a good café where your bike can have a post-ride hosedown while you tuck into coffee and cake. There are now also cabins and wigwams to rent on site, costing from £44 for two in high season.

On the B7062 to Traquair, see below, about two miles east from Peebles, is **Kailzie Gardens** ① *T01721-720007, Apr-Oct daily 1100-1730, Nov-Mar 1100-1700, £3*, with a walled garden, greenhouses, woodland walks, trout fishing pond, CCTV coverage of nesting ospreys nearby and an excellent courtyard restaurant.

Eight miles southwest of Peebles, a mile beyond the village of Stobo on the B712, is **Dawyck Botanic Gardens** ① *T01721-760254, mid Feb-mid Nov daily 1000-1800, till 1600 in Feb and Nov, £5.50, concession £4.50, £1 child*, an outstation of Edinburgh's Royal Botanic Garden, which contains a fine collection of trees and shrubs and landscaped wooded paths.

Peebles TIC ① *High St, T01721-723159, Apr-Oct daily, Nov and Dec hours vary.*

Riding of the Marches

The Border people's passion for rugby is matched only by their enthusiastic celebration of the Riding of the Marches, which takes place throughout the early summer months in each of the major towns. This ancient ritual dates back to the Middle Ages, when the young men – or 'Callants' – would ride out to check the boundaries of common lands owned by the town.

Each town has its own variations of the Riding ceremonies, with other activities including concerts, balls, and festivities lasting several days. Others also commemorate local historical events. For instance, the Selkirk Gathering, the oldest and largest of the Ridings, ends with the Casting of the Colours, which commemorates Scotland's humiliating defeat at the Battle of Flodden.

Innerleithen → *Phone code: 01896.*

Seven miles east of Peebles is the village of Innerleithen, home of **Robert Smail's Printing Works** ① *T0844-4932259 (NTS), mid-Mar-end Oct Thu-Mon 1200-1700, Sun 1300-1700, Nov-Dec Mon, Thu and Fri 1000-1600, Sat 0900-1500, £6.50, £5 child/concession*, on the main street, where you can see how printing was done at the beginning of the 20th century. You can watch the printer at work on the original machinery and even try your hand at typesetting.

There are many graded cycle routes through the Glentress, Cardrona and Elibank and Traquair forests, see www.7stanesmountainbiking.com. At **Walkerburn**, east of Innerleithen, you can link up to the fully signposted 90-mile **Tweed Cycleway**. See the tourist board leaflet *Cycling in the Scottish Borders*.

Traquair House → *Phone code: 01896.*

① *T01896-830323, www.traquair.co.uk, Apr-Sep daily 1100-170, Oct 1100-1600, Nov 1100-1500, £8, £7.20 concession, £4 child.*

The big attraction in these parts is the amazing Traquair House, one of Scotland's great country houses. It lies about a mile south of Innerleithen, on the south side of the Tweed. Traquair is the oldest continually inhabited house in the country and is still owned by the Maxwell Stuarts, who have been living here since 1491. Its history goes much further back, however, and parts of the house are believed to date from the 12th century. The original tower house was added to over the next five centuries, and most of what you see today dates from the mid-17th century. It has been visited by no fewer than 27 monarchs, including Mary, Queen of Scots, who stayed here with her husband, Darnley, in 1566. The place is steeped in Jacobite history, but the family paid for its Catholic principles. The fourth earl was imprisoned in the Tower of London, and sentenced to death, for his part in the Jacobite rising of 1715, but managed to escape with the help of his wife who smuggled him out disguised as a maid. The fifth earl served two years in the Tower of London for his support of Bonnie Prince Charlie in 1745 and the famous Bear Gates, which have remained closed ever since the Pretender passed through them on his way south, bear testament to his undying support. By the turn of the 18th century the family had lost most of its estates and had neither the money nor the motivation to undertake any major rebuilding.

As a result, visiting Traquair is genuinely like stepping back in time, and there's a uniquely nostalgic and spooky atmosphere missing from so many other historic houses. One of the most interesting rooms is the **priest's room**, where a succession of resident priests lived in hiding until the Catholic Emancipation Act of 1829 allowed them to give mass. Amongst the many fascinating relics is the cradle used by Mary, Queen of Scots for her son, James VI, and some letters written by the Stuart pretenders. Also worth seeing are the **gardens**, where you'll find a maze, craft shops, a cottage tearoom and an 18th-century working **brewery** producing several ales including Bear Ale and Jacobite Ale, which can be purchased in the tearoom and gift shop. There's also B&B accommodation available. A **craft and music fair** is held in the grounds of the house every August.

Galashiels → *Phone code: 01896. Population: 13,700.*

At the junction of the A72 and A7 Edinburgh-Carlisle road is the gritty, workmanlike textile town of Galashiels, strung out along the banks of the Gala River for more than two miles. Galashiels is one the largest towns in the Borders region, and a transport hub, but there's precious little to detain passing tourists. Galashiels has played a vital role in the Borders economy for over 700 years as a major weaving town, producing tartans, tweeds and woollens, and is the home of the **Scottish College of Textiles**, though the industry has gone into decline in recent times. **Galashiels TIC** ① *3 St John's St, T01896-755551, Apr-Jun and Sep-Oct Mon-Sat, daily Jul and Aug.*

Melrose and around → *For listings, see pages 47-52. Phone code: 01896. Population: 2300.*

Nestled at the foot of the mystical Eildon Hills, by the banks of the Tweed, is little Melrose, the loveliest of all the Border towns. It's an engaging mix of cute little shops and cottages and dignified Georgian and Victorian houses, and boasts one of the most famous ruins in Scotland. The normally soporific atmosphere is shattered every April during the week-long Melrose Sevens, when the town is taken over by rugby fans from all over the world for the acclaimed seven-a-side rugby tournament which has been going since 1883. Melrose makes a great base for exploring the beautiful landscapes of the middle stretch of the Tweed which so inspired Sir Walter Scott, the famous son of the Borders. Two of the area's main sights, Dryburgh Abbey and Abbotsford House, are inextricably linked with the writer's life and work. They can be reached by public transport, but you'll need your own transport if you want to get off the beaten track.

Places in Melrose
The bitter wars that ravaged the Scottish borders for centuries did irrevocable damage to **Melrose Abbey** ⓘ *T01896-822562 (HS), Apr-Sep daily 0930-1730, Oct-Mar daily 0930-1630, £5.50, £4.40 concession, £3.30 child*, but even in ruins it remains toweringly beautiful and impressive. It was founded in 1136 by the prolific David I (who helped to found all four of the great Border abbeys) and was the first Cistercian monastery in Scotland. It was attacked in 1322 by Edward II, but soon restored thanks to the financial assistance of Robert the Bruce. In 1385 it was largely destroyed by Richard II of England, then completely rebuilt, only to be ravaged again, this time by Henry VIII, in the mid-16th century. The abbey as it stands today dates from the 14th and 15th centuries, and was preserved by the money of the Duke of Buccleuch and the energy and talent of Sir Walter Scott. His great narrative poem *The Lay of the Last Minstrel* painted an eloquent picture of the abbey and helped him on the road to fame. The red sandstone ruins show an elaborate Gothic style and some of the finest figure sculpture in Scotland. Of particular note are the humorous gargoyles, which include a pig playing the bagpipes on the roof of the south side of the nave. The abbey's real claim to fame is that the **heart of Robert the Bruce** was buried here, at his request, after it had been taken to the Holy Land to help in the Crusades. The lead casket believed to contain the heart was finally excavated in 1996 and now takes pride of place in the abbey museum, in the **Commendator's House**, next to the church.

Next to the abbey is **Priorwood Garden** ⓘ *T01896-822493 (NTS), Mar-Oct Mon-Sat 1000-170, Sun 130-170, Nov-Dec Mon-Sat 1000-1600, £6.50, £4 concession, £16.50 family*, where plants are grown specifically for dried flower arrangements. There's also a dried flower shop on site. Also next to the abbey is **Melrose Tourist** ⓘ *Abbey St, T822555, daily Apr-Oct.*

On Market Square is the **Trimontium Exhibition** ⓘ *T01896-822651, Apr-Oct Mon-Sat 1030-1630, Sun 1400-1630, £2, £1.50 concession*, a small but interesting centre which tells the story of the Roman occupation of the area and includes some archaeological finds. The more adventurous can follow the **Trimontium Walk** ⓘ *T01896-822651, Apr-Oct Thu 1330-1700, £2*, a four-mile guided tour of Roman sites in the area, including the site of the Trimontium (Three Hills) fort at Newstead.

Eildon Hills
The three peaks of the Eildon Hills can be seen from all parts of the Central Borders region and can be climbed quite easily from Melrose. Starting from Market Square, head along the B6359 to Lilliesleaf, and after 100 yards the path is signed to the left and leads to the

Legends of the Eildons

The three-peaked Eildon Hills were considered a sacred place by the ancient Celts and have long been shrouded in mystery and associated with a number of legends. For a start, they are believed to have been created by the wizard/alchemist Michael Scott, and it was here that the mystic Thomas the Rhymer was given the gift of prophecy by the Faerie Queen. Most startling of all, though, is the claim that King Arthur and his knights lie asleep beneath the hills, victims of a terrible spell.

saddle between the North and Mid hills (Mid Hill is the highest, at 1385 ft). The path leads to the summit of North Hill, then Mid Hill, and finally West Hill, to the south. There are several routes back to town, but heading via the golf course makes a nice circular walk of two miles. Allow about 1½ hours. The route is detailed in the Eildon Hills Walk leaflet available from the tourist office.

St Cuthbert's Way

The 62-mile St Cuthbert's Way is a cross-border trail which links several places associated with St Cuthbert, who started his ministry at Melrose in the mid-seventh century and ended it at Lindisfarne (Holy Island), on the Northumberland coast. The waymarked route starts at **Melrose Abbey** and climbs across the Eildon Hills before joining the River Tweed. Highlights include Dere Street, a Roman Road, the Cheviot foothills, St Cuthbert's Cave and the causeway crossing to Lindisfarne. They can also provide a trail pack which includes maps and route descriptions.

Abbotsford House

ⓘ T01896-752043. *Visitor Centre and Gardens Apr-Sep daily 1000-1700, Oct-Mar 1000-1600; house daily Jul-Sep 1000-1700, Oct-Dec 1000-1600; house and gardens £8.75, £7.50 concession, £4.50 child, £28 family; garden only £3.50, £2.50 concession/child, £13 family.*

One of the Borders' top tourist attractions is Abbotsford House, home of Sir Walter Scott from 1812 to 1832 and a must for the novelist's many admirers. For an account of his life, see box, page 35. Scott spent a small fortune transforming the original farmhouse into a huge country mansion befitting a man of his status and, though Abbotsford may not be to everyone's taste, the house is an intriguing mix of styles and enjoys a beautiful setting. The house is still lived in by Scott's descendants, and the library and study have been preserved much as they were when he lived here, including the collection of over 9000 antiquarian books. There's also an amazing assortment of Scottish memorabilia, including Rob Roy's purse, Bonnie Prince Charlie's drinking cup and Flora MacDonald's pocketbook. The house is well worth visiting and sits in pleasant grounds, about three miles west of Melrose between the Tweed and the B6360. Take the Melrose-Galashiels bus and get off at the Tweedbank traffic island. From there it's a 15-minute walk.

Dryburgh Abbey

ⓘ T01835-822381, *Apr-Sep daily 0930-1730, Oct-Mar Mon-Sat 0930-1630 £5, £4 concession, £3 child.*

Five miles southeast of Melrose on the B6404, near the village of St Boswells, is Dryburgh Abbey. Its setting amongst ancient cedars on the banks of the Tweed makes it the most beautifully idyllic, romantic and evocative of the Border abbeys. It dates from around 1150,

Sir Walter Scott

Sir Walter Scott, a writer forever associated with the Borders, not only ruled the roost of his native Scotland but the world of literature in general. Born in 1771, the son of a wealthy Edinburgh lawyer, Scott spent much of his childhood in the Borders during which time he immersed himself in tales and ballads of Jacobites and Border heroes, giving him a passion for history which would infuse his later work.

It was this material which would eventually become poems in his three volumes of *Minstrelsy Of The Scottish Border* which established his name as a literary figure. Other romantic poetic works followed, such as *The Lady Of The Lake*, as with Burns, employing the Scottish dialect.

In 1811 Scott purchased Abbotsford, a farmhouse near Melrose (see page 34),

and during the following years developed the style which would remain his best-remembered contribution to literature, the historical novel. Collectively known as the Waverley novels, these included *Old Mortality*, *Rob Roy* and *The Heart Of Midlothian*. The original Waverley was a romantic tale of the Jacobite Rebellion of 1745 and the Highland society of the time. By 1819 Scott had moved beyond purely Scottish history and wrote *Ivanhoe*, set in 12th-century England. It remains his most enduring work, and he followed it with *Kenilworth*, *Redgauntlet* and *The Talisman*.

Scott died in ill health on 21 September 1832. His huge popularity was believed to have kept the spirit of Scotland alive and he is commemorated by the Scott Monument in Princes Street, Edinburgh.

---

when it was founded by Hugh de Morville for Premonstratensian monks from Alnwick in Northumberland. The 12th- and 13th-century ruin is remarkably well-preserved and complete, and was chosen as the burial place for Sir Walter Scott. His final resting place is in the north transept of the church. Close by lies Field Marshal Earl Haig, the disastrous First World War Commander.

If you're travelling by public transport from Melrose, take the **Jedburgh** bus as far as St Boswells (10 minutes), then walk north from the village for about a mile. If you're driving, make sure you pass **Scott's View**, on the B6356, which offers a sweeping view of the Eildon Hills and Tweed valley. Scott came here many times to enjoy the view (hence its name) and to seek inspiration. There's an even better view from the hill on the other side of the road.

Thirlestane Castle

North of Melrose on the main A68 is the stolid market town of **Lauder**, which merits inclusion because of **Thirlestane Castle** ① *T01578-722430; May, Jun, Sep Thu-Sun, Jul-Aug Wed-Sun, house 1000-1500, grounds till 1700; £9 house and grounds, £7 concession, £4 child, £20 family; grounds only £3, £3 concession, £1.50 child*, one of Scotland's oldest and finest castles, which stands on the eastern edge of town. The castellated baronial house is the seat of the Earls of Lauderdale and has been owned by the Maitland family since the 16th century. Inside, the 17th-century plaster ceilings are particularly notable.

Selkirk and around → *For listings, see pages 47-52. Phone code: 01750. Population: 6000.*

About six miles southwest of Melrose, on the A7 to Hawick, is the little town of Selkirk, standing on the edge of the Ettrick Forest which rises steeply from the Ettrick Water. Selkirk has been a textile centre since the early 19th century when the growing demand for tweed could no longer be met by the mills of Galashiels. Those mills are closed now and Selkirk is a quiet, unassuming place that only comes to life during the **Selkirk Gathering** in June, the largest of the Border Ridings, see box, page 31. That said, Selkirk is handily placed for visiting the other Border towns and sights, and makes a good base for touring the area.

Places in Selkirk
Halliwell's House Museum and Robson Gallery ① *T01750-20096, daily Apr-Oct Mon-Sat 1100-1600, Sun 1200-1500, free*, features an 18th-century ironmongers and tells the story of the town and its industry. The gallery has a changing programme of temporary exhibitions. Also on Market Square is **Walter Scott's Courtroom** ① *Apr-end Sep Mon-Sat 1000-1600, Jun-Aug also Sun 1400-1600, Oct Mon-Sat 1300-1600, free*, where Sir Walter Scott served as Sheriff of Selkirk from 1799 to 1832. It houses an exhibition on his life and writings. Outside the courtroom is a statue of the great novelist, and at the other end of the High Street is a statue of **Mungo Park** (1771-1805), the famous explorer and anti-slavery campaigner who was born in Selkirkshire.

At the northern end of town, on the A7 to Galashiels, is **Selkirk Glass** ① *T01750-20954, Visitor Centre Mon-Sat 0900-1700, Sun 1100-1700, Glass making Mon-Sat 0900-1630, Sat 1100-1500, free*, a thriving local industry, where you can see glass-blowing displays. **Selkirk TIC** ① *Market Sq, T01750-20054, daily Apr-Oct*, is next to Halliwell's House.

Bowhill House and Country Park
① *T01750-22204, www.bowhill.org, Estate open daily Apr-Sep (closed Tue Easter and Jul-Aug), House accessed by guided tour only, check website for dates.*
Three miles west of Selkirk, where the B7009 turns south off the A708, is the entrance to Bowhill House and Country Park, home of the Scotts of Buccleuch and Queensberry since 1812. They were once the largest landowners in the Borders and fabulously wealthy, a fact made evident by the fantastic collection of French antiques and European paintings on display. There are works by Canaletto, Guardi, Reynolds and Gainsborough. The wooded hills of the Country Park can be explored via a network of footpaths and cycle trails. There's no public transport to Bowhill, but the weekly Harrier Scenic Bus Service runs near Bowhill from Selkirk and Melrose in the morning, returning in the afternoon. It runs from July to September, see page 29.

Yarrow Water and Ettrick Water → *OS Landranger Nos 73 and 79.*
The A707 heads southwest from Selkirk to Moffat, following the beautiful Yarrow Water to **St Mary's Loch**, where the road is crossed by the Southern Upland Way. A few miles west of Selkirk is the turning south on to the B7009 which follows the course of the Ettrick Water to meet the B709, which continues south, past the village of **Ettrick** to Eskdalemuir and on to Langholm, see page 39.

This is one of the most remote and beautiful parts of Scotland, and an area inextricably linked with **James Hogg** (1770-1835), 'The Ettrick Shepherd', who was a great friend of Sir Walter Scott. Hogg was a notable writer himself and his most famous work, *The Confessions of a Justified Sinner*, is important in Scottish literature. Hogg was born in Ettrick and spent his entire life in the Ettrick and Yarrow valleys. He and Scott would often meet in **Tibbie Shiels Inn**, see Where to stay, page 48. From **Tibbie Shiels Inn** you can follow the Southern Upland Way south to Ettrick Water, where an unclassified road leads east to the village of Ettrick, or continue southwest all the way down to Moffat, see page 57. Alternatively, head north along the eastern shore of St Mary's Loch to the A708, then continue north to **Traquair House**, see page 31, then east towards Yair Hill Forest, where you can turn south to the **Broadmeadows Youth Hostel**, see Where to stay, page 48. These are strenuous hikes and you should be fit and well equipped.

At **Cappercleuch**, on the west shore of St Mary's Loch, a spectacular single-track road twists and turns its way up to the Megget Reservoir and then down past the Talla Reservoir to the tiny village of **Tweedsmuir**, on the A701, see page 57.

Jedburgh → *For listings, see pages 47-52. Phone code: 01835. Population: 4000.*

Ten miles from the English border is the attractive little town of Jedburgh, straddling the Jed Water at the edge of the northern slopes of the wild, barren Cheviot Hills. Jeburgh was strategically the most important of the Border towns, due to its proximity to England, and as a result received the full brunt of invading English armies. These days the only invaders are tourists. Jedburgh is the most visited of the Border towns and there are a number of interesting sights.

Arriving in Jedburgh
Jedburgh TIC ① *Murray's Green, T01835-863170, Apr, May and Oct Mon-Sat 1000-1700, Sun 1100-1600, Jun and Sep Mon-Sat 0930-1800, Sun 1100-1700, Jul and Aug Mon-Fri 0900-2000, Sat 1000-1900, Sun 1000-1800, Nov-Mar Mon-Sat 1000-1700, hours may vary*, is a large and well-stocked office with leaflets detailing local walks.

Places in Jedburgh
The town is dominated by **Jedburgh Abbey** ① *T01835-863925 (HS), Apr-Sep daily 0930-1730, Oct-Mar daily 0930-1630, £5.50, £4.40 concession, £3.30 child*, founded in 1138 by David I for Augustinian canons from northern France. The site had much older religious significance, however, and stonework in the abbey's museum dates from the first millennium AD. Malcolm IV was crowned here and Alexander III married his second wife in the abbey in 1285. Their wedding feast was held at nearby Jedburgh Castle (see below) and, like the castle, the abbey came under attack during the many English invasions, most devastatingly in 1523 when it was bombarded and burned. Despite this, the abbey church is remarkably complete, particularly the tower. Excavations have recently uncovered the remains of the cloister buildings, and among the finds is the priceless 12th-century 'Jedburgh comb', which is on display in the excellent visitor centre which brilliantly tells the abbey's long and fascinating history.

Nearby, at the top of the Castlegate, is **Jedburgh Castle Jail and Museum** ① *T01835-863254, end Mar-end Oct Mon-Sat 1000-1630, Sun 1300-1600, free*, which was formerly the county jail. It was built in 1823 on the site of the 12th-century castle, which changed hands many times until it was destroyed by the Scots because of its value to the English. The displays in the cell blocks depict prison life in the 19th century, and there's an exhibition on the town's history.

At the other end of the town centre is **Mary, Queen of Scots House** ① *T01835-863331, Mar-Nov Mon-Sat 1000-1630, Sun 1200-1630, free*, a beautiful 16th-century building of rough-hewn stone which contains a small bedroom occupied by Mary during her stay at Jedburgh in 1566. She spent several weeks here recovering from illness after her famous 30-mile ride to Hermitage Castle, see page 39, to visit her injured lover, the Earl of Bothwell. The ensuing scandal was only exacerbated by the murder of her husband Darnley the following year at Holyrood Palace in Edinburgh. Many years later, during her long incarceration, Mary regretted the fact that she hadn't died while staying in Jedburgh. This episode in Scottish history is told through a series of displays, and there are various artefacts associated with Mary.

Hawick and around → *For listings, see pages 47-52. Phone code: 01450. Population: 15,700.*

Hawick (pronounced 'Hoyk'), 14 miles southwest of Jedburgh and 12 miles south of Selkirk, is the largest town in the Borders and centres of the region's knitwear and hosiery industry for over 200 years. Hawick is not a place noted for its great beauty, but it does attract lots of visitors who come to shop at its many factory outlets where you can buy all the classic brand names in knitwear. A list of knitwear suppliers is available at the TIC.

Arriving in Hawick
Hawick TIC ① *Tower Mill, Heart of Hawick Campus, Kirkstile, T01450-373993, Easter-May and Oct Mon-Sat 1000-1700, Sun 1200-1700, Jun and Sep Mon-Sat 1000-1730, Sun 1200-1730, Jul and Aug Mon-Sat 1000-1800, Sun 1200-1800. Hours may vary.*

Places in Hawick
At 1 Tower Knowe is the Borders Textile Towerhouse, which tells the story of the regions' proud heritage in knitwear and tweed and also features a **fashion catwalk and design studio** ① *T01450-377615, textiletowerhouse@scotborders.gov.uk, Apr-Oct Mon-Sat 1000-1630, Sun 1200-1500, Nov-Mar Mon and Wed-Sat 1000-1600, closed Tue and Sun, free.* In Wilton Lodge Park is the **Hawick Museum and Scott Art Gallery** ① *T01450-373457, Apr-Sep Mon-Fri 1000-1200 and 1300-1700, Sat, Sun 1400-1700, Oct-Mar Mon-Fri 1200-1500, Sat closed, Sun 1300-1500, free*, which has an interesting collection of mostly 19th-century textile exhibits.

Around Hawick
The A7 runs southwest from Hawick through the dramatic scenery of Teviotdale to the tiny village of **Teviothead**, where it then exchanges the valley of the River Teviot for the **Ewes Water**. The Ewes then meets the River Esk at **Langholm**, in Dumfries and Galloway. The A7 continues its route south, to meet the A74(M) just north of Carlisle.

A much more beautiful route south is to take the A698 northeast out of Hawick, then turn off on to the A6088 which heads southeast. Just beyond the tiny village of **Bonchester Bridge**, take the B6357 which leads you into lovely **Liddesdale**. The B6357 follows the course of the Liddel Water all the way south to the village of **Canonbie**, see page 56, where it meets the A7.

A few miles north of Newcastleton, the B6357 meets the B6399 which runs north back to Hawick. Four miles north of the junction is the turning to **Hermitage Castle** ① *T01387-376222 (HS), Apr-Sep daily 0930-1730. £4, £3.20 concession, £2.40 child*, one of the great Border strongholds. The oldest part of the castle dates from the 13th century and it was in the hands of the Earls of Douglas until 1492, when it passed to the Earls of Bothwell. The fourth Earl of Bothwell, James Hepburn, was the third husband of Mary, Queen of Scots, following the murder of her second husband, Darnley, and is thought to have been behind the plot to murder him. It was to Hermitage that Mary made her famous ride to visit her future husband who had been injured in a border raid. Mary's marriage to Bothwell in 1566 was ill-advised and only succeeded in uniting their enemies; and led ultimately to her imprisonment in Lochleven Castle. Bothwell meanwhile fled to Norway, where he was captured and later died a prisoner himself, in 1578. Hermitage became largely irrelevant following the Union of Crowns in 1603 and fell into disrepair. Much of what you see today dates from the 19th century when the Duke of Buccluech ordered its repair. The vast and eerie ruin is said to be haunted, which is not surprising given its grisly past. One owner, William Douglas, starved his prisoners to death in the ghoulish dungeons, which can still be seen. There is no public transport service from Hawick to the castle.

Kelso and around → *For listings, see pages 47-52. Phone code: 01573. Population: 6000.*

The little market town of Kelso, at the confluence of the Tweed and Teviot rivers, is one of the most picturesque of the Border towns, with its cobbled streets leading into a wide market square bounded by elegant, three-storey 18th- and 19th-century town houses. The countryside around Kelso is worth exploring, for here you'll find some of Scotland's finest stately homes.

Places in Kelso

Kelso Abbey ① *Apr-end Dec daily (Sun afternoon only), free*, was once the largest and richest of the Border abbeys, but suffered the same fate as its counterparts, Jedburgh, Dryburgh and Melrose. Kelso was a strategic point in the Border wars between the Scots and the English and the abbey, founded in 1138 by King David, was laid to waste by successive English invasions, most devastatingly in 1545 by the Earl of Hertford. This latter attack was part of Henry VIII's so-called 'Rough Wooing', when the king took exception to the Scots' refusal to ratify a marriage treaty between his son and the infant Mary Stuart. Today, little remains of the abbey, and it is the least complete of those in the Borders. The nearby octagonal **Old Parish Church**, built in 1773, is unusual.

Aside from the abbey, the town's only other major attraction is the pleasant **Cobby Riverside Walk**, which leads along the banks of the Tweed to Floors Castle (see below). Leave The Square by Roxburgh Street, and follow the signposted alley to the start of the walk. The route passes the junction of the Tweed and Teviot rivers, a spot famous for its salmon fishing.

Kelso tourist information centre ① *Town House, The Square, T01573-228055, daily Apr-Oct*. Hours subject to change.

Kirk Yetholm and Town Yetholm

Six miles southeast of Kelso on the B6352 are the twin villages of Kirk Yetholm and Town Yetholm, lying within a stone's throw of the English border on the edge of the Cheviot Hills. Two long-distance walks cut through the villages. They are at the northern end of the Pennine Way, which runs up the spine of northern England, and are on the St Cuthbert's Way, which runs from Melrose to Lindisfarne in Northumberland, see page 34.

Floors Castle

① *T01573-223333, www.roxburghe.net, open Easter weekend and May-Sep 1030-1700, Oct 1030-1530; house and gardens £8.50, £7.50 concession, £4.50 child, £22.50 family; gardens only £4.50, £4 concession, £2 child.*

The vast ancestral home of the Duke of Roxburghe stands imperiously overlooking the Tweed, about a mile northwest of the town centre. The original Georgian mansion was designed by Robert Adam and built in 1721-1726, though it was later remodelled by William Playfair in the 1840s, with the addition of many flamboyant features. Only 10 rooms are open to the public but they are undeniably elegant and palatial, and amongst the many priceless family items on display are outstanding collections of European furniture, porcelain and paintings by Picasso, Matisse and Augustus John, and a 15th-century Brussels tapestry. Floors is the largest inhabited castle in Scotland and the current occupier, the 10th Duke of Roxburghe, is a close personal friend of the royal family. The house also has a restaurant and a coffee shop.

Smailholm

Six miles northwest of Kelso on the B6397 is the village of Smailholm, where a turning leads to **Smailholm Tower** ⓘ *T01573-460365 (HS), Apr-Sep daily 0930-1730, Oct-Mar Sat, Sun 0930-1630, £4.50, £3.60 concession, £2.70 child,* a classic Scottish tower house and an evocative place full of history and romance. The 15th-century fortified farmhouse, built by the Pringles, squires to the Earls of Douglas, stands on a rocky pinnacle above a small lake. Sir Walter Scott's grandfather owned the nearby farm and the young Scott came here as a sickly child in the 1770s to improve his health. So began the writer's long love affair with the lore and landscapes of the Scottish Borders which inspired so much of his poetry and prose. Scott would write a ballad about this gaunt tower house – *The Eve of St John* – as part of a deal with the owner to save it. Today Smailholm houses a small, unremarkable museum relating to some of Scott's works, but the views from the top of the tower are rewarding.

Mellerstain House

ⓘ *T01573-410225, www.mellerstain.com, Easter weekend and May-Sep Fri-Mon 1230-1700, last admission 1630, café/gardens 1130-1730. House and gardens £8.50, £4 child, (under 5s free).*

Northwest of Kelso, on the A6089 to Gordon, is the signpost for Mellerstain House, home of the Earl of Haddington and one of Scotland's great Georgian houses. This 18th-century architectural masterpiece was designed by William Adam and his son Robert and perfectly characterizes the elegant symmetry of the period. The superb exterior is more than matched by the exquisitely ornate interiors. There is also furniture by Chippendale and Hepplewhite, as well as paintings by Constable, Gainsborough, Veronese and Van Dyck. The formal Italian gardens, laid out in the early 20th century, are equally impressive.

Coldstream → *Phone code: 01890.*

Standing on the north bank of the River Tweed, which marks the border with England, is the little town of Coldstream. The busy A697 linking Newcastle-upon-Tyne with Edinburgh runs through the centre of town, but Coldstream has little to offer visitors other than history. The town gave its name to the famous regiment of Coldstream Guards, formed by General Monck in 1659 before he marched south to support the restoration of the Stuart monarchy a year later. The regiment had originally been sent to Scotland as part of Cromwell's New Model Army, but Monck was persuaded to change allegiance. No doubt the offer of the title, first Duke of Albermarle, had something to do with his decision. The Guards remain the oldest regiment in continuous existence in the British army and you can find out all about their proud history in the **Coldstream Museum** ⓘ *T01890-882630, Market Sq, off the High St, Apr-Sep Mon-Sat 1000-1600, Sun 1400-1600; Oct Mon-Sat 1300-1600, free.*

Near the handsome five-arched bridge which spans the river at the east end of town is the 18th-century **Toll House**, where eloping couples from England were once granted 'irregular marriages'. On the western edge of town is the 3000-acre **Hirsel Country Park** ⓘ *open all year during daylight hours,* seat of the Earls of Home. Hirsel House isn't open to the hoi polloi, but you can wander around the grounds.

Coldstream Tourist Information Centre ⓘ *Town Hall on the High St, T01890-882607, Apr-Jun and Oct Mon-Sat, daily Jul-Aug. Winter hours vary.*

Flodden Field

Four miles southeast of Coldstream, across the border near the village of Branxton, is Flodden Field. In 1513 James IV crossed the Tweed at Coldstream to attack the English, while Henry VIII was busy fighting in France. The invasion was a diversion to assist the French, but Henry sent an army north to meet the threat and James IV's army was routed. The king, his son and some 9000 men were slain in one of Scotland's greatest military disasters.

Not such a Dunce

Duns was also the birthplace of John Duns Scotus (1266-1308), a medieval scholar and theologian of some note, who taught at the universities of Oxford and Paris. He opposed the orthodox views of Thomas Aquinas, and his teachings divided the Franciscans and Dominicans. After his death his ideas quickly fell out of favour and those who held them were derided as being stupid, and so we now have the word 'dunce', derived from the heterodox views of John Duns Scotus.

Duns and around → *For listings, see pages 47-52. Phone code: 01361.*

The quiet market town of Duns lies in the middle of Berwickshire, surrounded by the fertile farmland of the Merse. Duns is best known as the birthplace of Jim Clark (1936-1968), a former farmer who went on to become world motor racing champion twice in the 1960s and who remains one of Britain's greatest ever racing drivers. His successful career was tragically cut short when he was killed in a crash while practising at Hockenheim in Germany.

The **Jim Clark Room** ① *44 Newton St, T01361-883960, Apr-Sep Mon-Sat 1000-1300 and 1400-1630, Sun 1400-1600, Oct Mon-Sat 1300-1600, free*, is a museum dedicated to this motor racing champion's life.

There are some good local walks, detailed in the leaflet *Walks Around Duns*. The best walk is to the top of **Duns Law** (714 ft), from where there are terrific views of the Merse and the Lammermuir Hills to the north. Also at the top is the **Covenanter's Stone**, which marks the spot where the Covenanting army camped in 1639, awaiting the arrival of Charles I's troops. Duns Castle was used for many of the Highland scenes in the film, *Mrs Brown*.

Duns lies only a few miles south of the **Lammermuir Hills**, a low-lying range running east to west and acting as a natural boundary between the Borders and East Lothian. The hills are criss-crossed by numerous paths and ancient droving trails, including the easterly section of the **Southern Upland Way** from Lauder, on the A68, to Cockburnspath by the A1 on the coast. You can walk the final 10 miles of the route, starting from the hamlet of **Abbey St Bathans**, northwest of Duns on the Whiteadder Water.

Two miles east of Duns, on the A6015, is **Manderston House** ① *T01361-883450, www. manderston.co.uk, mid-May to Sep Thu and Sun 1330-1700, gardens 1130-dusk; house and gardens £9, £8.50 concession, £5 child (under 12s free); gardens only £5, £4.50 concession, £2.50 child (under 12s free)*, described as the finest Edwardian country house in Scotland. No expense has been spared in the design and decoration and the whole effect, from the silver staircase to the inlaid marble floor in the hall, is one of quite staggering opulence. Take a good look at the staircase – it had tarnished badly over the years (one panel is left to show how black it was) and was voluntarily and lovingly cleaned up by a retired couple. The 56 acres of beautiful gardens should not be missed. There are wonderful displays of rhododendrons late in May.

Twelve miles east of Duns, and five miles west of Berwick-upon-Tweed off the B6461 to Swinton, is **Paxton House** ① *Easter-Oct daily 1100-1700, gardens 1000-dusk, £7.60, £7 concession, under 16s free; gardens only £4, £2.50 concession, under 16s free*, a grand neoclassical mansion designed by John and James Adam, the less-famous brothers of Robert, for Patrick Home, who had fallen in love with a Prussian aristocrat at the court of Frederick the Great. She was a great favourite of Frederick's and he strongly opposed the marriage, which never went ahead. She and Patrick corresponded for years and vowed never to marry anyone else while the other was alive. Both kept their promise. Inside there's an impressive display of Chippendale and Regency furniture, and the Picture Gallery is an outstation of the National Gallery of Scotland. In the 80 acres of grounds beside the River Tweed is a Victorian boathouse and a salmon-fishing museum.

The Berwickshire Coast is not exactly a name on the tip of every Scottish tourist's tongue. Tucked out of the way, these wild and woolly cliffs are often deserted and home to a number of excellent coastal walks, particularly the seven-mile Burnmouth to St Abbs walk described below. The waters around Eyemouth are excellent for scuba diving. They form part of the St Abbs and Eyemouth Voluntary Marine Reserve, one of the best dive sites in Scotland, with a wide variety of marine life and the spectacular Cathedral Rock.

Eyemouth → *Phone code: 01890. Population: 3500.*

Five miles north of the border on the Berwickshire Coast is the busy fishing port of Eyemouth. Fishing has been the life and soul of Eyemouth since the 13th century and the **Eyemouth Museum** ① *T01890-751701, www.eyemouthmuseum.org, Apr-Oct Tue-Sat 1000-1600, Sun 1200-1600, £3.50 £3 concession, under 16s free,* in the Auld Kirk on Market Place, has displays on the town's fishing heritage. The centrepiece is the Eyemouth Tapestry, made by local people in 1981 to mark the centenary of the Great Disaster of 1881, when 189 local fishermen were drowned during a violent storm. **Eyemouth TIC** ① *T01890-750678, daily Apr-Sep, Oct Mon-Sat, hours subject to change,* is in the same building as the museum.

St Abb's Head → *Phone code: 01890.*

Three miles north of Eyemouth on the A1107 is the village of **Coldingham**, notable only for its medieval **priory**, founded by King Edgar in 1098, then rebuilt in the 13th century before suffering further attacks in 1545 and 1648. The remaining sections have been incorporated into the present parish church. Here the B6438 turns north and winds its way down to the picturesque little fishing village of St Abbs, nestled beneath steep cliffs. There's a little museum and a visitor centre for the Marine Reserve in the Old School House – open summer, hours vary with volunteer staff. St Abbs is also a good base for divers wishing to explore the St Abbs and Eyemouth Voluntary Marine Reserve, see below.

Just north of the village is the **St Abb's Head National Nature Reserve** (NTS), which comprises almost 200 acres of wild coastline with sheer cliffs inhabited by large colonies of guillemots, kittiwakes, fulmars and razorbills. To get to the reserve, follow the trail from the car park at Northfield Farm on the road into St Abbs. The path ends at the lighthouse, about a mile from the car park. An excellent coastal walk, from Burnmouth, south of Eyemouth, to St Abbs is described below. A side road turns off the B6438 at Coldingham and leads a mile down to the coast at **Coldingham Sands**, a tiny resort with a fine sandy beach. It's a popular spot for surfing and diving.

Burnmouth to St Abbs coastal walk → *OS Landranger No 67.*

The Berwickshire Coast offers some good walking opportunities along high cliffs with lots of birdlife to see. This walk starts at **Burnmouth**, a few miles south of Eyemouth. To get there, take the hourly bus service from Coldingham, which connects in Berwick with services to other Border towns. The seven-mile route is waymarked and is mostly on good paths, though there is some rough ground. Allow about four hours and take care at some points along the clifftop. To get to the cliff path, get off the bus at Burnmouth primary school, go through the gate by the houses and walk up the side of the field. Continue along the path towards Eyemouth, past some dramatic scenery at **Fancove Head**, the highest point of the cliffs, at 338 ft. When you reach the golf course, follow the signs around the seaward edge and then left across the golf course, then right towards **Eyemouth harbour**.

Cross the bridge near the lifeboat mooring and walk along the quayside to the end of the promenade, where you cross a short section of beach and then climb the steps to the headland and the remains of Eyemouth Fort. Walk around the seaward side of the Caravan Park and turn right to cross the fields and then return to the cliff path. The path descends to **Linkum Shore** and crosses the beach. Follow it around Yellow Craig to reach **Coldingham Bay**. At the far end of the bay, climb the steps and then follow the tarmac path which leads to the village of **St Abbs**. From here you can follow Creel Path to reach the B6438, and from there it's a short walk into Coldingham.

Berwick-upon-Tweed → *Phone code: 01289.*
Yes, we know, Berwick-upon-Tweed is in England, but the town has strong historical ties with Scotland, and its football team plays in the Scottish league. It also makes a convenient stopping point if you've had a long journey north. The town, which takes its name from a river which has its source in Scotland, wasn't always in England. It changed hands more than a dozen times between 1147 and 1482, when it was finally taken for England by Richard, Duke of Gloucester, later Richard III. Berwick was a strategic base for English attacks on the Borders and large sections of the town wall, built by Edward I to repel the Scots, still survive. It has also retained its medieval street plan, and many of its steep, cobbled streets are worth exploring. The **TIC** ① *106 Marygate, T01289-330733, Oct-Mar Mon-Sat 1000-1200 and 1300-1600, longer hours from Easter to Oct.*

Scottish Borders listings

For hotel and restaurant price codes and other relevant information, see pages 12-19.

😊 Where to stay

Peebles and the Tweed Valley *p30*

££££ Cringletie House Hotel, T01721-730233, www.cringletie.com. 2 miles north of Peebles just off the A703 to Edinburgh. Lovely 19th-century baronial house set in 28 acres of grounds, with an excellent restaurant, see page 50, and friendly service.

££££ Peebles Hotel Hydro, Innerleithen Rd, Peebles, T01721-720602, www.peebles hotelhydro.co.uk. One of Scotland's oldest and grandest hotels, the Hydro has made a concerted effort to meet modern demands with an excellent pool and a health and beauty suite offering a huge range of therapies. Also provides a whole host of activities for kids and baby-sitting service. Prices include dinner in the grand, but rather formal dining room. Their bistro, **Lazels**, is more relaxed. Various deals on offer so best to call and ask for the best prices.

££££ Stobo Castle Health Spa, Stobo, 7 miles outside of Peebles, T01721-725300, www.stobocastle.co.uk. This luxury hotel housed in an early 19th-century baronial castle offers more than 70 treatments for face and body, as well as an exercise pool complex and high-tech gym, and various exercise and relaxation activities. Above all, though, it's a great place to unwind or even meditate. Plenty of special offers available but prices don't include treatments.

£££ Castle Venlaw Hotel, on the Edinburgh Rd, T01721-720384, www.venlaw.co.uk. Lovely old baronial castle with excellent facilites and service and good views.

£££ Horse Shoe Inn, at Eddleston, about 5 miles north of Peebles on the A703, T01721-730225, www.horseshoeinn.co.uk. Restaurant with rooms. Very classy and comfortable place to stay and serves very good food. See also Restaurants, page 50.

£££ Kingsmuir House, Springhill Rd, Peebles, T01721-724413, www.kingsmuirhouse.co.uk. 2 rooms. Small, luxurious Victorian B&B, friendly, close to town centre.

£££-££ Traquair Arms Hotel & Restaurant, Traquair Rd, Innerleithen, T01896-830229, www.traquairarmshotel.co.uk. Good place to stay and a local favourite for its fine food and real ales. Also has self-catering cottages for rent.

££ Glentress Hotel and Country Inn, at the entrance to Glentress Forest, T01721-720100. Cosy, bike-friendly place with a good restaurant.

££ Rowanbrae, Northgate, which runs off the east end of the High St, Peebles, T01721-721630. Open all year. Excellent B&B.

Camping

Rosetta Caravan & Camping Park, on Rosetta Rd, a 15-min walk north of the High St, Peebles, T01721-720770. Open Apr-Oct.

Tweedside Caravan Park, Montgomery St, Innerleithen, T01896-831271. Open Apr-Oct. Note that accommodation is usually fully booked during the **Traquair Fair** in late Jul/Aug.

Melrose and around *p33*

There's not a huge amount of accommodation in Melrose, considering its appeal, so it's best to book in advance during the summer and especially during the Melrose Sevens in mid-Apr. The following options are all in Melrose.

£££ Burts Hotel, Market Sq, T01896-822285, www.burtshotel.co.uk. This refurbished traditional 18th-century inn is the best option, very comfortable and renowned locally for its excellent modern Scottish cuisine, see Restaurants, page 50.

£££ Townhouse Melrose, Market Sq, T01896-822645, www.thetownhouse melrose.co.uk. Small, stylish and and comfortable hotel run by the same family who own the Burts Hotel. Good food in the restaurant or brasserie.

££ Braidwood, Buccleuch St, T01896-822488, www.braidwoodmelrose.co.uk. Another good choice of B&B. Very good value.

££ Kilkerran House, High St, T01896-822122, www.kilkerran.net. One of the best B&Bs in the centre. Nicely furnished and also offers good food.

£ Youth Hostel, in a large mansion on the edge of town, overlooking the abbey from beside the A6091 bypass, T01896-822521, Open all year. Very good and very popular.

Camping
Gibson Park, T01896-822969, at the end of the High St, the campsite is opposite the Greenyards rugby ground.

Selkirk and around p36
£££ Philipburn Country House Hotel, Linglie Rd, Selkirk, T01750-720747, www.bw-philipburnhousehotel.co.uk. Part of Best Western chain with all the facilities you'd expect. Upmarket accommodation and good food.

£££-££ Glen Hotel, Yarrow Terr, Selkirk, T01750-20259, www.glenhotel.co.uk. Refurbished and very comfortable Victorian house with good views of the hills and river. Popular with golfers and fishermen. Dog friendly.

£££-££ Tibbie Shiels Inn, T01750-42231. Beautifully situated on the narrow strip of land separating St Mary's Loch from the ethereal Loch of the Lowes. It's still a famous watering hole and popular stop along the Southern Upland Way. It also serves meals in its dining room and the cosy bar is good for a pint of ale or a wee dram.

££ Gordon Arms Hotel, east of St Mary's Loch, at the junction of the A708 and B709 which runs north to Innerleithen and south and then east to Hawick, T01750-82232. Said to be the last meeting place of Scott and Hogg. It's a popular stopping point for

walkers, and offers bar food and local ales as well as frequent live folk music. Refurbishing their rooms at the time of going to press.

££ Hillholm, 36 Hillside Terr, Selkirk, T01750-21293. Good value. 5 mins' walk from town.

££ Sunnybrae House, 75 Tower St, Selkirk, T01750-21156. Dinner also available. Bedrooms with adjoining private sitting room.

£ SYHA Broadmeadows Youth Hostel, Yarrowford, T01750-76262. Open end Mar to end Sep, 5 miles west of Selkirk on the A708, beyond Bowhill (see below).

Camping
Victoria Park Caravan & Camping Site, Selkirk, T01750-20897. Beside the river next to the indoor swimming pool.

Jedburgh p38
£££ Jedforest Hotel, in the village of Camptown, 6 miles south of Jedburgh, on the A68, and only 5 miles from the border, T01835-840222. This is the most luxurious place to stay. It is the self-proclaimed 'First Hotel in Scotland' and is very comfortable, with a fine restaurant. Price is for dinner B&B.

££ Ancrum Craig, T01835-830280, www.ancrumcraig.co.uk. Open Jan-Dec. A quiet 19-century country house 2 miles from the A68 near Ancrum. Great value.

££ Hunalee House, T01835-863011. Open Mar-Oct. There are several B&Bs in and around town, but few can match the sheer style and value-for-money of this early 17th-century house, a mile south of town on the A68, set in 15 acres of gardens and woodlands.

££ Kenmore Bank B&B, Oxnam Rd, T01835-862369, www.kenmorebank.com. Overlooking the Jed Water in town. Stylish and comfortable B&B.

££ Meadhon House, 48 Castlegate, Jedburgh, T01835-862504, www.meadhon. com. More characterful than most. Friendly and welcoming B&B.

Camping

There are a few campsites close to Jedburgh.
Elliot Park Camping & Caravanning Club, a mile north of town, T01835-863393. Open Apr-Oct.
Jedwater Caravan Park, 4 miles south of town on the A68, T01835-840219. Open Apr-Oct.
Lilliardsedge Holiday Park and Golf Club, 5 miles to the north of Jedburgh, T01835-830271. Open Easter-end Oct.

Hawick and around *p39*

£££ Mansfield House Hotel, 1 mile from town, on the A698 to Kelso, T01450-373988, www.themansfieldhousehotel.com. A traditional mansion house hotel offering good food (lunch **£**; dinner **££**).
£££-££ Glenteviot Park, Hassendeanburn, Hawick, T01450-870660. 5 rooms. Purpose-built hotel overlooking the Teviot River, faultless design and exceptional service, strictly for grown-ups in search of some indulgence and pampering.
£££-£ 3 Liddesdale Hotel, Newcastleton, 5½ miles south of Hermitage Castle, T01387-375255. Comfortable, friendly small hotel with restaurant serving local specialities such as pheasant and salmon.

Kelso and around *p40*

££££ Ednam House Hotel, Bridge St, Kelso, T01573-224168, www.ednamhouse. com. Less salubrious then the Roxburghe but nevertheless highly recommended and slightly more affordable. A family-run Georgian mansion overlooking the Tweed and close to the town centre. Excellent food served all day (lunch **££**; dinner **£££**) in a restaurant with great views over the river.
££££ Roxburghe Hotel & Golf Course, at the village of Heiton, a few miles from Kelso on the A698 to Hawick, T01573-450331, www.roxburghe.net. This country mansion, owned by the Duke of Roxburgh, is the most luxurious place to stay hereabouts. It stands in hundreds of acres of park and woodlands on the banks of the Teviot, and offers grand

style, superb cuisine and a championship golf course.
£££-££ Border Hotel, T01573-420237, www.theborderhotel.com. Kirk Yetholm, overlooking the village green, which marks the end of the Pennine Way. Kirk Yetholm was once the home of the king of the gypsies (you can still see his pretty little cottage by the green) and the bar is full of pictures of the former gypsy inhabitants. It serves a welcome pint of ale and good food, too.
££ Bellevue House, Bowmont St, Kelso, T01573-224588, www.bellevuehouse.co.uk. Fine non-smoking guest house.
££ Valleydene, High St, Kirk Yetholm, T01573-420286. Cosy B&B with log fire in guest lounge.
£ Youth Hostel, Kirk Yetholm, T01573-420631. Open mid-Mar to end Oct.

Camping

Kirkfield Caravan Park, Grafton Rd, Town Yetholm, T01573-420346, open Apr-Oct. A caravan park, does not take tents.
Springwood Caravan Park, T01573-224596, admin@springwoodcaravanpark.co.uk. Open Mar-Oct. Overlooking the Tweed on the A699 heading west towards St Boswells, this is the nearest campsite to Kelso.

Duns and around *p43*

££££-£££ Chirnside Hall Hotel, a mile east of Chirnside on the road to Berwick, T01361-818219, www.chirnsidehallhotel.com. This Victorian mansion house offers luxurious accommodation and excellent food all day at mid-range prices (booking essential).
££ St Albans, T01361-883285, on Clouds, a lane behind the police station in Duns. Recommended and non-smoking.

Berwickshire Coast *p45*

££££ Churches, Albert Rd, Eyemouth, T01890-750401, www.churcheshotel.co.uk. 6 rooms. Such a serious wow factor is suprising here. Stylish without a hint of pretension. The restaurant, see page 51, is the best for miles.

£££ Marshall Meadows Country House Hotel, Berwick-upon-Tweed, T01289-331133, www.marshallmeadowshotel.co.uk. Georgian mansion set in 15 acres of grounds only a few hundred yards from the border. Highly recommended.

£££-££ Dunlaverock Guest House, at Coldingham Sands, T01890-771450. A small, comfortable guesthouse offering excellent food.

££ Castle Rock Guest House, Murrayfield, on the cliffs above the harbour in St Abbs Head, T01890-771715. Excellent.

£ Youth hostel, Coldingham Sands, on the cliffs above the south end of the bay, T01890-771298. Open mid-Mar to end Sep.

Camping

Eyemouth Holiday Park, T01890-751050. Overlooking the beach at the north end.

Scoutscroft Holiday Centre, St Abb's Head, T01890-771338. Open Mar-Nov. Also rents diving equipment and offers courses. One of several campsites in the area.

Restaurants

Peebles and the Tweed Valley p30

£££-££ Cringletie House Hotel, see Where to stay, page 47. Open 1230-1400, 1900-2100. The best place to eat. It serves delicious Scottish cuisine.

££ Horse Shoe Inn, Eddleston, about 5 miles north of Peebles on the A703, T01721-730225. Excellent food sourced locally. Lunch ££ and dinner £££. See also Where to stay, page 47.

££ The Sunflower Restaurant, 4 Bridgegate, T01721-722420, www.sunflowerrestaurant. co.uk. A great place in the centre of Peebles which serves coffee, cakes and Mediterranean style lunches – as well as evening meals on Thu, Fri and Sat.

£ The Olive Tree, 7 High St, Peebles. An excellent deli in town selling a wide selection of continental delicacies and local produce and specializes in cheeses.

Melrose and around p33

£££ Burt's Hotel, see Where to stay, page 47. Best of all. Dine in style in the dining room or opt for their excellent pub grub.

£££ Townhouse Melrose, Market Sq, T01896-822645, www.thetownhouse melrose.co.uk. Run by the same family who own the **Burts Hotel** and food is just as good, whether eating in the restaurant or the less formal brasserie.

£££-££ Hoebridge Inn Restaurant, on the other side of the river, in the village of Gattonside, T01896-823082, www. hoebridgeinn.com. Offers good quality Scottish fare, and well worth the walk.

£££-££ Marmions Brasserie, T01896-822245, on Buccleuch St near the abbey. French-style bistro serving superb food daily 0900-1800, 1830-2200. Believed by some to be the best place to eat in the region, and it has the awards to back it up.

Selkirk and around p36

Possibilities for eating in Selkirk are limited.

££ County Hotel, on the High St, T01750-21233, www.countyhotelselkirk.co.uk. Serves decent bar meals.

£ Jackie Lunns, Market Sq, Selkirk. Buy the local speciality, Bannock bread, from here.

Jedburgh p38

There's not a great deal of choice for eating in Jedburgh or Hawick, apart from the hotel bars and restaurants.

££ Carter Bar, 11 miles south of Jedburgh, is notable for being the first/last pub in Scotland, standing on the border with England in the Cheviot Hills.

££-£ Simply Scottish, High St, Jedburgh, T01835-864696, www.simplyscottish.co.uk. Offers modern, bistro-style Scottish fare all day.

Kelso and around p40

£££-££ Roxburghe and **Ednam House Hotels**, see Where to stay, page 49. Far and away the best places to eat.

££ Queens Head, 24 Bridge St, Kelso, T01361-224636, www.queensheadhotel kelso.com. Its Courtyard Bar is a decent place in which to grab a bite.
£ Black Swan Hotel, on Horsemarket, T01361-224563, www.theblackswanhotel. co.uk. Offers simple, unfussy foods.

Duns and around p43
£££ Wheatsheaf at Swinton, in the village of Swinton, about 5 miles south of Duns on the A6112, T01361-860257, www. wheatsheaf-swinton.co.uk. Open Tue-Sun 1200-1400, Tue-Sat 1800-2100. The best place to eat in the area. The food is first-class.

Berwickshire Coast p45
£££ Churches, Albert Rd, Eyemouth, T01890-750401. Run by Rosalind and Marcus, who also have the eponymous hotel, see Where to stay, page 49. Superior cooking served with aplomb in chic surroundings. Dishes feature local fish and game.
££ Northfield Farm Visitor Centre, a good place to eat if you're going to St Abb's Head. Has a pleasant tea room with tables outside.
££-£ The Ship Hotel, Eyemouth, T01890-750224, www.shiphoteleyemouth.co.uk. Best of a string of pubs and hotels along the harbour serving fresh fish and standard bar meals.

🎭 Entertainment

Melrose and around p33
The Wynd Theatre, T01896-823854. A tiny theatre which stages regular drama.

✷ Festivals

Jedburgh p38
Jedburgh's Common Riding, the Callant's Festival, takes place in **late Jun/early Jul**, see also box, page 31.
In **early Feb** is the **Jedburgh Hand Ba' game**, a bruising and exhausting contest between the 'uppies' (those born above the Market Place) and the 'downies' (those born

below), who endeavour to get a leather ball from one end of the town to the other. Visitors from south of the border may wish to note that the game used to be played with the heads of vanquished Englishmen.

Kelso and around p40
The main festivals are the **Border Union Agricultural Show** and the town's **Riding of the Marches**, both of which take place in **Jul**. Kelso also hosts its own **Rugby Sevens** in early **Sep**.

Berwickshire Coast p45
The main events in Eyemouth's calendar naturally has a fishing theme. The week-long **Herring Queen Festival** takes place late **Jul**.

⏱ What to do

Jedburgh p38
Ferniehirst Mill Lodge, 2 miles south of Jedburgh on the A68, T01835-863279, www.ferniehirstmill.co.uk. Horse riding is available for experienced riders here. They also offer accommodation and tailor-made riding holidays.

Berwickshire Coast p45
There are a number of boats offering dive charters as well as birdwatching boat trips.
Pathfinder Boat Charters, T01890-771525, www.stabbsdiving.com.
Alternatively ask down at the harbour. All based in St Abb's Head.
Scoutscroft Holiday Centre, T01890-771669, www.scoutscroft.co.uk. See Where to stay, page 50. Dive shop here which rents out equipment and runs diving courses.

🚍 Transport

Peebles and the Tweed Valley p30
There are hourly buses from Peebles to **Edinburgh** (1 hr), **Galashiels** and **Melrose** and, less frequently, to **Selkirk** and **Biggar**, with First Edinburgh, T01721-720181. Buses stop outside the post office, near the TIC,

on Eastgate. Bus No C1 runs once a day to **Traquair** from **Peebles**. First Edinburgh, T01721-720181, bus No 62 runs regularly to **Innerleithen** and **Peebles** from **Edinburgh**. From **Galashiels** there are frequent buses to and from **Edinburgh** (1 hr 25 mins); **Peebles**, **Melrose** (20 mins), **Hawick** (40 mins), **Selkirk** (15 mins) and **Carlisle** (2 hrs).

Melrose and around *p33*
From Melrose there are regular buses to **Galashiels** (15 mins), **Kelso** (several daily; 35 mins), **Jedburgh** (30 mins), **Peebles** (several daily; 1 hr 10 mins), and **Selkirk** (hourly Mon-Sat, less frequently on Sun; 40 mins). To get to **Hawick**, it's easier to catch a bus to Galashiels and then change (see page 29). Buses to Melrose stop in Market Square, close to the abbey and tourist office. First Edinburgh bus No 95 runs frequently to and from **Edinburgh** and **Hawick**, via **Selkirk** and **Galashiels**. There are also regular daily buses to **Langholm** and **Carlisle**. There's a bus to **Moffat**, on Sat only. All buses leave from Market Sq.

Selkirk and around *p36*
See Melrose, above, for details.

Jedburgh *p38*
The bus station in Jedburgh is close to the abbey and there are good connections around the Borders. First Edinburgh, T0131-6639233, runs frequent daily buses to **Hawick**, **Kelso** and **Galashiels**. There are also buses daily to and from **Edinburgh**. From **Hawick** there are regular daily buses to and from **Selkirk** (20 mins), **Edinburgh** (2 hrs) and **Carlisle** (1¼ hrs). There's also a service to **Melrose** (40 mins), but it may be quicker to go to **Galashiels** and change there.

Kelso and around *p40*
Kelso bus station is on Roxburgh St, a short walk from The Square. There are regular buses to and from **Galashiels**, **Melrose**, **Jedburgh**, **Coldstream** and **Kirk Yetholm** (20 mins). Services are less frequent on Sun. For more details, contact the main bus operator **First Edinburgh**, T0131-663 9233, or Traveline, T0870-6082608. There are also several buses (Mon-Sat) to and from **Berwick-upon-Tweed** which pass through **Duns** and **Coldstream**.

Berwickshire Coast *p45*
There are several buses daily to **Eyemouth** from **Edinburgh** (1 hr 40 mins), and there are a couple of daily buses (Mon-Fri) to and from **Kelso**, via **Duns**. There's also a daily service to and from **Berwick-upon-Tweed**. First Edinburgh, T01896-752237, and Swan's Coaches, T01289-306436. Buses between **Edinburgh** and **Berwick-upon-Tweed** pass through **Coldingham** several times daily. There's also an hourly service between **St Abbs**, **Coldingham**, **Eyemouth** and Berwick. Traveline, T0870-6082608.

Berwick is on the main **London–Aberdeen** rail line and there are fast and frequent trains to and from Edinburgh.

If you're driving, the best route north is the scenic A1107 which joins the fast A1 near Cockburnspath.

ℹ Directory

The main border towns all have banks, post office, petrol stations and a decent range of shops, as well as internet access in the local library, details of which are available from the TICs.

Contents

Footprint features

Dumfries & Galloway

Dumfries and Galloway

Dumfries and Galloway is one of Scotland's forgotten corners, forsaken by most visitors for the cities of Edinburgh and Glasgow or the grandeur of the Highlands. But the southwest has much to offer those prepared to leave the more-beaten track. Away from the main routes west from Dumfries to Stranraer and north to Glasgow, traffic and people are notable by their absence, leaving most of the region free from the tourist crush of more popular parts. Some of the most beautiful scenery is to be found along the Solway Coast, west from Dumfries to the Mull of Galloway. Here you'll find the romantic ruins of Caerlaverock Castle, Threave Castle and Sweetheart Abbey, along with Whithorn Priory, known as the 'Cradle of Christianity' in Scotland. Also on this lovely coast is the beguiling town of Kirkcudbright, inspiration for some of Scotland's most famous artists and still a thriving artistic colony. Rising behind the coastline are the Galloway Hills which form part of the 150,000-acre Galloway Forest Park, a vast area of mountains, moors, lochs and rivers, criss-crossed by numerous trails and footpaths suitable for all levels of fitness. Running right through the heart of the Galloway Hills is the 212-mile Southern Upland Way, one of the country's great long-distance walks, see page 71. The southwest also has strong literary associations. The great poet, Robert Burns, lived and died here, in Dumfries, and the town boasts several important Burns sights.

Arriving in Dumfries and Galloway

Getting there and around

The region has a good network of buses. The main operators are **Stagecoach West Scotland** ① www.stagecoachbus.com, and **MacEwan's** ① T01387-710357. **National Express** ① www.nationalexpress.com, has long-distance coaches from London, Birmingham, Glasgow and Edinburgh to Stranraer, for the ferry crossing to Belfast and Larne in Northern Ireland. There are two train routes from Carlisle to Glasgow, via Dumfries and Moffat. There's also a line from Stranraer to Glasgow. For rail information, www.nationalrail.co.uk. Dumfries and Galloway council has a travel information website, www.dumgal.gov.uk for all public transport services. ▶▶ For further details, see Transport page 77.

Tourist information

Dumfries and Galloway Tourist Board ① 64 Whitesands, T01387-253862, www.visitdumfriesandgalloway.co.uk, has its head office in Dumfries. They have a range of free brochures and guidebooks for the region, including accommodation, birdwatching, cycling, fishing, walking and golfing. There are also tourist offices in Stranraer, Castle Douglas, Gatehouse of Fleet, Gretna Green, Kirkcudbright, Moffat and Newton Stewart.

Annandale, Eskdale and the Lowther Hills → For listings, see pages 72-79.

Cutting through the eastern reaches of Dumfires and Galloway is the A74(M), the congested main route from England to Scotland. Most people whizz straight through this area on their way north, but away from the main roads there are a few interesting places to visit.

Gretna Green → Phone code: 01461.

The first place you encounter across the border is the nondescript little village of Gretna Green. It's not a particularly interesting place to visit, but Gretna Green has been synonymous with marriage ceremonies for many years and thousands of couples still come here to tie the knot. **World Famous Old Blacksmith's Shop** ① T01461-338224, www.gretnagreen.com, Apr-Jun daily 0900-1800, Sep daily 0900-1900, Jul and Aug daily till 2000, Oct-Mar 0900-1730, £1.50, under 12s free, houses a visitor centre with a small exhibition on Gretna Green's history as well as gift shops. Opposite is the tourist office which opens daily. There's also the rival **Gretna Hall Hotel** ① www.gretnaweddings.co.uk, where better-off runaway couples would come to maintain a class distinction.

Ecclefechan and Lockerbie → Phone code: 01576.

Nine miles northwest of Gretna Green on the A74(M) is the neat little village of Ecclefechan, birthplace of the great writer and historian **Thomas Carlyle** (1795-1881), one of the most powerful and influential thinkers in 19th-century Britain. His old home, The Arched House, is now a tiny museum known as **Carlyle's Birthplace** ① T0844-4932247, Easter and Apr-30 Sep Fri-Mon 1200-1600. £3.50, £2.50 concession, £9 family, and features a collection of personal memorabilia.

About eight miles north of Ecclefechan is **Lockerbie**, a quiet, unassuming little town which hit the headlines on 21 December 1988 when a Pan-Am jumbo jet, flying from Frankfurt to New York, was blown up by a terrorist bomb, killing all 196 passengers and crew. The plane's fragments fell on the town, killing a further 11 people. After many months of exhausting diplomatic efforts, the two suspects were extradited from Libya,

Wedding bellows

In Scotland, a marriage declaration made before two witnesses used to be legally binding, and anyone could perform the ceremony. This meant that eloping couples from south of the border came to Scotland to have their weddings witnessed by whomever came to hand. As Gretna Green was the first available community on the main route north, it became the most popular destination for runaway lovers. In their desperation, many tied the knot at the first place to hand after getting off the stagecoach, and in Gretna this happened to be the local blacksmith's shop, situated at the crossroads. The marriage business boomed in the village, until 1940 when marriage by declaration was made illegal. However, under Scots law young couples can still marry at 16 without parental consent, and Gretna Green still attracts its fair share of Romeos and Juliets.

tried in a Scottish court set up in the Netherlands, and sentenced to life imprisonment, though later released on grounds of ill health. But for the people of Lockerbie life has never been the same.

Langholm → *Phone code: 01387.*
Langholm sits at the confluence of three rivers – the Esk, Lewes and Wauchope – on the A7, one of the main routes north to Edinburgh, and a less stressful alternative to the A74(M). During the 18th century Langholm became a thriving textile town and is still a major centre of the Scottish tweed industry. This is clan Armstrong country and the **Clan Armstrong Trust Museum** ① *T01387-380610, www.armstrongclan.org.uk, Easter-mid Oct Fri-Sun, Tue and Wed 1400-1700, free*, is a must for anyone with that particular surname. Neil was here, but we don't think Lance would be particularly welcome.

Langholm was also the birthplace of the great **Hugh McDiarmid** (1892-1978), poet and co-founder of the Scottish National Party. He is also buried here, against the wishes of the local nobs, who took great exception to his radical views. On the hill above the town is the **McDiarmid Memorial**, a stunning modern sculpture which looks like a giant metallic open book. A path leads for about half a mile to another memorial, from where there are wonderful views across the Southern uplands and the Solway Firth. A signed single-track road leads off the A7, about half a mile north of Langholm, to a path which leads to the memorials.

North from Langholm

The A7 runs north to Hawick and on to Edinburgh. It also runs south to Carlisle, via **Canonbie**, through an area known as the Debatable Land until the border was settled in 1552. From Canonbie, the B6357 provides a more scenic alternative route to the Borders running through lovely **Liddesdale** towards Hawick and Jedburgh, see page 39. A shorter route to Liddesdale is to take the single-track road heading east off the A7 just to the north of Langholm, which joins the B6357 at Newcastleton.

Another scenic route from Langholm to the Borders region is the B709. It runs northwest to the tiny village of **Eskdalemuir**, 14 miles from Langholm, then north through the Eskdalemuir and Craik forests to **Ettrick**, where it follows the valley of the Ettrick Water to Selkirk, see page 36. About 1½ miles north of Eskdalemuir is the **Kagyu Samye Ling Tibetan Monastery** ① *T01387-373232, www.samyeling.org, temple open for* *visitors daily 0600-2100, tearoom and shops daily 0900-1700.* This Tibetan Buddhist centre was founded in 1967 for study, retreat and meditation, and incorporates the Samye Temple, the first Tibetan Buddhist monastery in the west. Visitors are free to wander round the temple and peace garden and a programme of retreats and weekend courses is available, as well as accommodation. There's also a café for vegetarian meals (pre-booking advised) and shops on site and pleasant walks through the gardens. Bus No 112 from Lockerbie stops at the centre.

Moffat → *Phone code: 01683. Population: 2000.*

Just to the east of the A74(M), at the northern end of Annandale, is the neat and tidy market town of Moffat. Once a fashionable spa town, Moffat is now a centre for the local woollen industry, as clearly evidenced by the statue of a ram on its wide High Street. The **tourist information centre** ① *T01683-220620, daily Apr-Oct,* is on Ladyknowes, off the A701 heading into town from the A74. It has a selection of leaflets detailing the many local walks. Near the TIC is the **Moffat Woollen Mill** ① *T01683-220134, Mar-Oct daily 0900-1730, Nov-Feb daily till 1700, free,* where you can see a demonstration of traditional weaving and trace your Scottish ancestry. There's also a shop selling woollens and tartans. Nearby is the **Moffat Museum** ① *T01683-220868, Easter to end Sep Mon, Tue and Thu-Sat 1030-1300 and 1430-1700, Sun 1430-1700, £1, £0.20 child,* which tells the town's eventful history.

Around Moffat

Moffat makes a convenient base from which to explore the Lowther Hills to the west and the wild and barren southwest Borders to the east, either by car or on foot. The A708 to Selkirk is a very beautiful route which passes through the most stunning parts of the Southern Uplands. Ten miles northeast of Moffat on this road is the spectacular **Grey Mare's Tail** waterfall, which plunges 200 ft from a glacial hanging valley. It's only a five-minute walk from the car park up a series of steps to the base of the falls. More serious walkers can take the path which crosses the stream and climbs steeply up to **Loch Skeen**, the source of the falls. It's about an hour to the loch. From Loch Skeen experienced walkers can climb to the summit of **White Coomb** (2696 ft). This is also a popular birdwatching area. The A708 carries on into the Borders region and passes the famous **Tibbie Shiels Inn**, see Where to stay, page 48, on the shores of **St Mary's Loch**, see page 36.

Another scenic route from Moffat is the A701 which runs north towards Edinburgh. En route it meets the A72, which heads east to Peebles and along the Tweed Valley, see page 30. Six miles north of Moffat on the A701 you get a great view of the **Devil's Beef Tub**, a vast, deep natural bowl once used by Border *reivers* (rustlers) for hiding stolen cattle. The Tub was also used as a hide-out by persecuted Covenanters during Charles II's 'killing times'.

Further north the road enters **Tweeddale** and passes through tiny **Tweedsmuir**, where a spectacular side road climbs up into the hills to meet the A708 at St Mary's Loch, see page 36. Just to the north of Tweedsmuir is the historic **Crook Inn**. The old country inn has strong literary associations. **Robert Burns** wrote his poem *Willie Wastle's Wife* in what is now the bar, and Sir Walter Scott used to pay the occasional visit. From the inn you can climb **Broad Law** (2756 ft), the second highest hill in southern Scotland.

Biggar → *Phone code: 01899.*

North of Moffat, is the old market town of Biggar, just across the regional border, in South Lanarkshire. Biggar stands on the A702, the main route from the M74 to Edinburgh, and makes a pleasant and convenient stopping-point for those driving to the capital from the south. The town centre has had a recent makeover and there are enough places of interest to warrant a few hours here. The **tourist information centre** ① *155 High St, T01899-221066, Easter-Sep Mon-Sat 1000-1700, Sun 1200-1700.*

Moat Park Heritage Centre ① *T01899-221050, Easter-Oct Mon-Sat 1100-1630, Sun 1400-1630, closed Wed. £2.50, £2 concession, £1.50 child*, is housed in a renovated church near the foot of Kirkstyle, off the High Street. It includes displays on local history, archaeology and geology as well as some very interesting tapestries. Ask here about details of **Hugh McDiarmid's Cottage**, which is three miles north of town. It was the home of the poet until his death and can be viewed by appointment only.

There are four other museums in Biggar. Close by, on North Back Road, is **Gladstone Court Museum** ① *same times and admission prices as Moat Park above*, which features a Victorian street with shops, a bank and schoolroom preserved just as they were 150 years ago. The Gladstone family, ancestors of the 19th-century Liberal Prime Minister, William Ewart Gladstone, are buried in the churchyard of St Mary's Church. **Greenhill Covenanters' Museum** ① *T01899-221050, open 1st Sat of month May-Sep or by appointment 1400-1630, £1.50, £1.20 concession, £1 child*, on Burnbrae, traces the development of the Covenanting movement. Nearby is the **Gasworks Museum** ① *Jun-Sep daily 1400-1700, £1, £0.50 concession*, the only surviving coal-fired gasworks in Scotland. On Broughton Street is the **Puppet Theatre** ① *T01899-220631, www.purvespuppets.com*, set up by Purves Puppets, a touring theatre company. There are regular workshops, backstage tours and shows are held all year round in the Victorian theatre.

Biggar is overlooked by **Tinto Hill** (2333 ft), near the village of Symington, four miles southwest of town at the junction of the A72 and A73. It's a fairly easy walk from the village to the summit, from where the views are fantastic. There's also a Druidic Circle and Bronze-Age burial cairn. A good track starts from near the Tinto Hill farm shop on the A73. Allow about three hours. Regular Biggar-Lanark buses pass through Symington.

The Lowther Hills

West of Moffat, between the A74(M) and Nithsdale, are the wild and bare Lowther Hills. About 13 miles north of Moffat, at Elvanfoot, the B7040 leaves the A74(M) and crosses the hills, passing through the old lead-mining villages of Leadhills and Wanlockhead to meet the A76 a few miles south of Sanquhar, see page 62.

Leadhills is a rather forlorn-looking place, but a few miles south is **Wanlockhead**, the highest village in Scotland at 1500 ft and home of the **Museum of Lead Mining** ① *T01659-74387, www.leadminingmuseum.co.uk, Easter to end Sep daily 1100-1630, £7.75, £5.70 concession/child, £24.75 family*. The visitor centre gives an introduction to the mining industry and there's a guided tour of an old lead mine, miners' cottages and the 18th-century library. Wanlockhead was also a gold mining centre and you can try your hand at gold panning at the museum. From Leadhills **Britain's highest adhesion railway** ① *T01555-820778, www.leadhillsrailway.co.uk, £3.50, £1.50 child*, runs to Wanlockhead every hour from 1100 till 1600, passing through the old mine workings.

Dumfries is the largest town in southwest Scotland, straddling the River Nith, a few miles from the Solway Firth. Known as the 'Queen of the South', Dumfries has long been a thriving market town and seaport for a large agricultural hinterland, and its strategic position made it a prime target for English armies. Its long history of successive invasions began in 1306, when Robert the Bruce committed the first act of rebellion against Edward I by capturing Dumfries Castle, which led to the Wars of Independence. But it was town planners in the 1960s who did more to destroy the town centre than invading armies. Nevertheless, Dumfries is a pleasant and convenient base from which to explore the beautiful Solway Coast, and its associations with Robert Burns, who spent the last years of his life here, also make it worth a visit in its own right. There are many interesting sights lying within easy distance of Dumfries, including Caerlaverock Castle to the southeast,

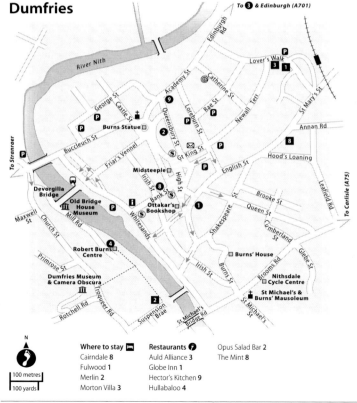

Dumfries

Where to stay 🛏
Cairndale **8**
Fulwood **1**
Merlin **2**
Morton Villa **3**

Restaurants 🍴
Auld Alliance **3**
Globe Inn **1**
Hector's Kitchen **9**
Hullabaloo **4**

Opus Salad Bar **2**
The Mint **8**

Drumlanrig Castle to the north in Nithsdale as well as some of the best mountain biking trails in Scotland, particularly in Mabie Forest, south of town on the road to New Abbey.

Arriving in Dumfries

Getting there and around The bus station is a short walk west of the High Street, at the top of Whitesands beside the river. The train station is on the east side of town, a five-minute walk from the centre. If driving, there's parking by the river opposite the TIC. Collect a disc from the TIC for three hours' free parking. For all bus times, check **Traveline Scotland** ① *www.travelinescotland.com*. ▸▸ *For further details, see Transport page 77.*

Tourist information TIC ① *64 Whitesands, on the corner of Bank St, T01387-253862. Apr, May and Oct daily 1000-1700, Jun-Sep daily 0930-1800.*

Places in Dumfries

Most of the town's attractions and facilities are on the east side of the river. A tour of the main sights should begin on the pedestrianized High Street, at the **Burns Statue**, at its northern end. It shows the great bard sitting on a tree stump with his faithful dog at his feet. A few minutes' walk along the High Street is the **Midsteeple**, built in 1707 to serve as a courthouse and prison. Nearby, at 56 High Street, is the **Globe Inn**, one of Burns' regular drinking haunts, where you can sit in the poet's favourite chair and enjoy a drink, see Bars and clubs, page 76. Continue down the High Street and follow the signs for **Burns' House** ① *T01387-255297, Apr-Sep Mon-Sat 1000-1700, Sun 1400-1700, Oct-Mar Tue-Sat 1000-1300, 1400-1700, free*, in Burns Street, where the poet spent the last few years of his life, and died in 1796. It contains some interesting memorabilia, including original letters and manuscripts. Just to the south is the red sandstone **St Michael's Church**. In the churchyard is the **mausoleum** where Burns lies buried. Pick up a copy of the free Burns Trail leaflet from the TIC.

On the other side of the river is the award-winning **Robert Burns Centre** ① *Mill Rd, T01387-264808, Apr-Sep Mon-Sat 1000-1700, Sun 1400-1700, Oct-Mar Tue-Sat 1000-1300 and 1400-1700, free, audio-visual £2, £1 concession*, housed in an old water mill. It tells the story of Burns' last years in the town. On the hill above, centred around an 18th-century windmill tower, is **Dumfries Museum** ① *T01387-253374, Apr-Sep Mon-Sat 1000-1700, Sun 1400-1700, Oct-Mar Tue-Sat 1000-1300 and 1400-1700, free*, which has good local history, natural history and anthropology displays. On the top floor of the windmill tower is a **Camera Obscura** ① *Apr-Sep, Mon-Sat 1000-1700, Sun 1400-1700, £2.30, £1.15 concession*. Also on the west bank of the river, at the west end of the 15th-century Devorgilla Bridge, is the dinky **Old Bridge House** ① *T01387-256904, Apr-Sep Mon-Sat 1000-1700, Sun 1400-1700, free*. Built in 1660 and the town's oldest house, it is now a rather disjointed museum.

On the outskirts of town is the **Dumfries and Galloway Aviation Museum** ① *Heathhall Industrial Estate, T01387-259546, www.dumfriesaviationmuseum.com, Easter-Oct Wed 1100-1600, Sat and Sun 1000-1700, Jul-Aug Wed-Fri 1100-1600, £4, £3 concession/ child, £12 family*, a diverting collection of old aircraft and memorabilia based around the original control tower of RAF Dumfries, and staffed by volunteers. It's all very hands-on and you can even sit in the cockpit of a jet fighter.

Caerlaverock Castle

ⓘ *T01387-770244 (HS), Apr-end Sep daily 0930-1730, Oct-Mar daily 0930-1630, £5.50, £4.40 concession, £3.30 child.*

Eight miles from Dumfries, on the east bank of the Nith estuary where it enters the Solway Firth, is the magnificent ruin of Caerlaverock Castle, the ultimate defensive fortress and one of the best-preserved medieval castles in Scotland. The unusual triangular-shaped castle, which dates from around 1277, was the stronghold of the Maxwells, the Wardens of the Western Marches. But though surrounded by a moat and impregnable-looking, it has fallen several times over the course of its long history. It was first besieged and captured in 1300 by Edward I of England during the Wars of Independence, then destroyed by Robert the Bruce. It was repaired in the 1330s, then 300 years later refurbished in the trendy Renaissance style by Robert Maxwell, first Earl of Nithsdale. But several years later it was attacked again, this time by the Covenanters, who captured it after a 13-week siege and proceeded to trash the place. Caerlaverock was never occupied again. A nature trail runs behind the castle and through the woods to the site of the original castle, built in the 1220's and abandoned within 50 years as it was too close to the salt marshes of the Solway Firth. There's also a siege exhibition, a gigantic model Trebuchet (a medieval siege engine) and café. Stagecoach Western bus No 371 travels by the castle from Dumfries.

A few miles further on is the **Caerlaverock Wetlands Centre** ⓘ *T01387-770200, www.wwt.org.uk, daily 1000-1700, £7.50, £5.70 concession, £3.70 child, £20.20 family, WWT members free*, the largest wetland reserve in Britain and an absolute must-see for birdwatchers. The 8000 ha of mudflats and merse attract many thousands of birds, most notably barnacle geese, migrating here in the winter. A series of hides and observation towers allow you to get very close to the birds, and during the summer months there are nature trails through wildflower meadows, where you may see the rare natterjack toad. There's also a visitor centre and a Fair Trade coffee shop.

Ruthwell

About seven miles east of Caerlaverock along the B724 is the turning to the little village of Ruthwell. Inside the village church is the remarkable **Ruthwell Cross** ⓘ *T01387-870249, free, key to church from Mrs Coulthard*, which dates from the late seventh century when the whole of southern Scotland and northern England, from the Humber-Mersey line to the Forth, was controlled by the Angles. The two main faces of the 18-ft high cross are carved with religious and secular figures and bear inscriptions in both Latin and runes. Bus No 79 passes through Ruthwell from Dumfries.

Mabie Forest

Four miles south of Dumfries is the turn-off to Mabie Forest, a large area criss-crossed by forest paths and mountain bike trails of varying degrees of difficulty. The nine-mile Rik's Red Route offers some of the best single track in the country. You can hire bikes at **Riks Bike Shed**, see page 78. They have a bike shop and café and the hugely enthusiastic and knowledgeable staff will advise on anything to do with cycling. They also have a hire-only site at Drumlanrig, see below. Mabie Forest is part of the 7 Stanes project, see www.7stanesmountainbiking.com.

West of Dumfries

Off the A75 to Castle Douglas, is **Glenkiln Reservoir**, where you'll find an extraordinary collection of sculptures scattered amongst the hills, woods and meadows of Glenkiln

Estate. There are six works in all, the easiest ones to find being *John the Baptist* by Rodin, which stands at the head of the reservoir, and *Standing Figure* by Henry Moore. There are other works by Moore as well as one by Epstein, which is hidden in a copse of Scots Pine. Heading west on the A75, take the turning right for Shawhead, about nine miles west of Dumfries. From Shawhead, follow signs for the reservoir.

Ellisland Farm

① *T01387-740426, www.ellislandfarm.co.uk, Apr-end Sep Mon-Sat 1000-1300 and 1400-1700, Sun 1400-1700, Oct-Mar Tue-Sat 1400-1700, £4, £3 concession, under 15s free.*
Six miles northwest of Dumfries, on the A76 at Hollywood, is Ellisland Farm. This was the home of Robert Burns from 1788 to 1791, during which time he built the farmhouse and tried to introduce new farming methods. Ultimately, this venture collapsed and he moved to Dumfries, but not before writing his famous ghost story, *Tam o' Shanter*, and Hogmanay favourite, *Auld Lang Syne*. The farmhouse is now a museum displaying various personal items.

North of Dumfries

About 14 miles north of Dumfries is **Thornhill**, where the A702 heads eight miles west to the peaceful little conservation village of **Moniaive**. Bus No 202 runs to Moniaive from Dumfries. Four miles north of Thornhill is the turning for **Drumlanrig Castle** ① *T01848-330248, www.drumlanrig.com, castle Easter to end Aug daily1100-16, gardens and parkland Easter-end Sep daily 100-1700, castle, gardens and parkland £10, £8 concessions, £6 child, £28 family, gardens and parkland only £6, £4.50 concession, £3.50 child, £16 family.* More French château than Scottish castle, this sumptuous stately home of the Duke of Buccleuch and Queensberry is renowned for its superb art collection, which reflects the mind-boggling wealth of its owners. Included are works by such luminaries as Rembrandt, Leonardo Da Vinci, Holbein, Breughel and Van Dyck, as well as numerous family portraits by Allan Ramsay and Godfrey Kneller. After all that you may need to clear your head with a stroll round the extensive country park. You can also hire mountain bikes and explore a network of trails. There's also a **bicycle museum** commemorating the fact that the bicycle was invented nearby, at Keir Mill.

Seven miles north of Drumlanrig, the B797 turns right (east) off the A76 and climbs up to **Wanlockhead**, the highest village in Scotland, see page 58. A few miles further, on the A76, is the neat little town of **Sanquhar**, which lies on the Southern Upland Way.

New Abbey and around → *Phone code: 01387.*

Seven miles south of Dumfries, in the endearing little village of New Abbey, are the graceful red sandstone ruins of **Sweetheart Abbey** ① *T01387-850397 (HS), Apr-end Sep daily 0930-1730, Oct daily 0930-1630, Nov-Mar Mon-Wed and Sat-Sun 0930-1630, £4, £3.20 concession, £2.40 child,* founded by Cistercian monks in 1273. The abbey gets its name from the extreme marital devotion of its patron, Lady Devorgilla de Balliol, wife of John, who founded Balliol College, Oxford. On his death she had his heart embalmed and carried it around with her, until her own death in 1290. Now both she and the heart are buried in the presbytery. The ruins can be appreciated just as easily from outside the perimeter fence, or even better, from the patio of the **Abbey Cottage tearoom**. New Abbey is dominated by **Criffel Hill** (1867 ft). One and a half miles south of the village take the turning for Ardwell Mains Farm, from where a track leads to the summit. The views from the top are magnificent, stretching all the way south to the lakes and across to the Borders.

A few miles south of New Abbey, at **Kirkbean**, is the turning for the **John Paul Jones Cottage** ⓘ *T01387-880613, Easter-end Sep Tue-Sun 1000-1700, Jul and Aug daily 1000-1700, £3.50, £3 concession, child free*, birthplace of the US naval hero. It's now a small museum and includes an exhibition and audio visual of his amazing life. While you're here don't miss a visit to the **Steamboat Inn**, see page 75, in the tiny hamlet of Carsethorn, at the end of the single-track road. South of Kirkbean, at **Southerness**, there's an excellent championship **golf course** ⓘ *T01387-880677*, overlooking Sandyhills Bay.

Rockcliffe and Kippford → *Phone code: 01556.*

The A710 turns west south of Kirkbean and parallels the Solway Coast, past the wide expanse of the perfectly named **Sandyhills Bay** to **Colvend**. About a mile beyond, a side road turns off to the impossibly cute little village of **Rockcliffe**, its row of whitewashed cottages facing a rocky cove and beach at the mouth of the Urr estuary. On a sunny day it's almost too perfect.

From Rockcliffe you can walk about 1½ miles to neighbouring **Kippford**, a popular sailing centre, along the **Jubilee Path** (NTS). The path passes the **Mote of Mark**, an ancient Celtic hillfort. Another path runs south from Rockcliffe along the cliff tops, to **Castlehill Point**. From Kippford, at low tide, you can walk across the causeway to **Rough Island**, a 20-acre offshore bird sanctuary owned by the NTS. During May and June, when the terns and oystercatchers are nesting, it's out of bounds.

Kirkcudbright, Castle Douglas and around → *For listings, see pages 72-79.*
Phone code: 01557. Population: 3500.

Kirkcudbright (pronounced 'kir-koo-bree') sits at the mouth of the River Dee and is, without doubt, the most attractive town in the southwest. It has an airy and spacious feel to it, its wide streets lined with elegant Georgian villas and Victorian town houses. The Glasgow Boys, see below, started to come here in the late 19th century and established an artists' colony, and ever since then Kirkcudbright has been a favourite haunt of artists – the Scottish equivalent of St Ives in Cornwall. Several miles northeast of Kirkcudbright, Castle Douglas couldn't be more different, geared as it is towards to more active outdoor pursuits such as cycling, golf and watersports on nearby Loch Ken.

Arriving in Kirkcudbright and Castle Douglas

Getting there and around Kirkcudbright, 25 miles west of Dumfries, can be reached via the A75 or A711. It is 50 miles east of Stranraer on the A75. Bus 500 runs between Dumfries and Stranraer passing through Castle Douglas and Newton Stewart. Bus Nos 501, 502 and 505 run between Kirkcudbright and Dumfries. ▸▸ *See Transport, page 77.*

Tourist information Kirkcudbright TIC ① *beside the harbour, T01557-330494, Apr-Jun, Sep and Oct 1000-1700; Jul and Aug 0930-1800*, will book accommodation for you during the busy summer season, and sell the leaflet *Walks Around Kirkcudbright*, which details many local walks. See also www.kirkcudbright.co.uk.

Kirkcudbright

Near the harbour is **MacLellan's Castle** ① *T01557-331856 (HS), Apr-end Sep 0930-1730, £4, £3.20 concession, £2.40 child*, which is a castellated town house rather than a defensive fortress. It was built in the 1570s by the then-provost, Thomas MacLellan of Bombie, using stone from the adjoining ruined monastery. The castle is relatively complete, except for the roof, and inside there's a warren of rooms to explore.

Nearby, at 12 High Street, is the wonderful **Broughton House** ① *T0844-493 2246 (NTS), house and garden open end Mar-end Oct daily 1200-1700, £6.50, concession £5, £16.50 family*, the Georgian town house which was bought in 1901 by E A Hornel, the renowned artist and member of the 'Glasgow Boys', an influential late 19th-century group of painters who established an artists' colony in Kirkcudbright. Many of Hornel's works are on display here, in the excellent **Hornel Gallery**. The artist also designed the beautiful **Japanese Garden**, which leads from the house down to the river.

Only a few minutes' walk along the High Street is the early 17th-century tolbooth, which now houses the **Tolbooth Art Centre** ① *T01557-331556, May, Jun, Sep Mon-Sat 1100-1700, Sun 1400-1700, Jul-Aug Mon-Sat 1000-1700, Sun 1400-1700, Oct Mon-Sat 1100-1600, Sun 1400-1700, Nov-Apr Mon-Sat 1100-1600, free.* As well as featuring a display of works by Hornel and his fellow 'colonists', including local artist Jessie King, the centre also tells the story of the town's artists colony from the late 19th century to the present day, and there are temporary exhibitions of local arts and crafts and photography. Another of the town's art galleries is the **Harbour Cottage Gallery**, which hosts a variety of shows throughout the year. From art to artefact, one of the town's more eclectic attractions is the **Stewartry Museum** ① *St Mary St, T01557-331643, May, Jun, Sep Mon-Sat 1100-17, Sun 1400-1700, Jul-Aug Mon-Sat 1100-1700, Sun 1400-1700, Oct, Mon-Sat 1100-1600, Sun 1400-1700, Nov-Apr Mon-Sat 1100-1600, free*, an extraordinarily diverse collection of exhibits

Hero and villain

John Paul Jones (1747-1792) was a hero to the Americans, but the British saw him as a pirate. Early on in his nautical career, as plain John Paul, he was imprisoned in Kirkcudbright Tolbooth for the manslaughter of his ship's carpenter. His fortunes changed, along with his name, in later life when he joined the US fleet in 1775. Four years later, during the American War of Independence, in command of a few American and French ships, he won a dramatic victory against a powerful British force off the English coast and became an American hero. He is generally regarded as the father of the modern US Navy.

reflecting the social and natural history of this part of the Solway coast, once known as the Kirkcudbright Stewartry because it was administered by the kings' stewards during the 14th and 15th centuries.

A few miles northwest of town, off the A75 at Twynholm, is a **museum** ① *T01557-860050, www.davidcoulthardmuseum.co.uk, Easter to end Oct daily 1000-1600, £4, £2 concession/child, £10 family*, dedicated to Formula 1 star **David Coulthard**, who was born in the area. The collection includes memorabilia from his go-carting days up to the present. There's a popular tearoom too called **The Pit Stop**.

Dundrennan Abbey and Orchardton Tower

About seven miles southeast of Kirkcudbright are the ruins of **Dundrennan Abbey** ① *T01557-500262 (HS), Apr-end Sep daily 0930-1730, Oct-Mar Sat and Sun 0930-1630, £4, £3.20 concession, £2.40 child*, a 12th-century Cistercian establishment standing in a beautifully bucolic setting in a secluded valley. You may not be too surprised to learn that the abbey has associations with Mary, Queen of Scots. She spent her last night on Scottish soil here. Although Bus No 505 travels between Kirkcudbright and Dumfries passing through Dundrennan, if you're feeling energetic, the better option is the lovely five-mile walk along quiet country roads.

A mile further east is the lovely wee village of Auchencairn and, between here and Palnackie, see Festivals, page 77, is the turn-off for the 15th-century **Orchardton Tower** ① *(HS) Apr-Sep daily 0930-1830, Oct-Mar Mon-Sat 0930-1630, free, key available locally*, the only circular tower house in Scotland. A few miles north of Palnackie is **Dalbeattie**, a distinctly unremarkable town but with a wide range of shops and services. Just south of Dalbeattie, off the A710 to Kippford, is the start of the notorious **Hardrock Trail**, a must for all mountain-bike enthusiasts and one of the 7stanes trails (www.7stanesmountainbiking.com).

Castle Douglas

The neat little town of Castle Douglas, standing on the edge of lovely little **Carlingwark Loch**, was laid out in the 18th century by Sir William Douglas, a local lad who made his fortune in the Americas. There's nothing of note in the town itself, but it makes a good alternative base for exploring Galloway Forest Park, see page 67, and the surrounding sights. The A713 runs north from Castle Douglas along the shores of long and skinny **Loch Ken**, a popular watersports centre, with sailing, windsurfing, water-skiing, canoeing, rowing and fishing, see What to do, page 77. There's also an RSPB nature reserve on the west bank, and walking trails. **Castle Douglas TIC** ① *Market Hill Car Park, T01556-502611, Apr-Jun, Sep and Oct daily 1000-1630, Jul and Aug daily 1000-1800*.

Threave Garden and Estate

ⓘ *T01557-502575 (NTS), gardens all year from 0930 till sunset; visitor centre Apr-Oct daily 1000-17000, Feb-Mar and Nov-Dec Fri-Sun 1000-1700; house Mar-Oct Wed-Fri and Sun 1100-1530, guided tours only, hours and garden £12, £8.50 concession, £28.50 family, garden only £6.50, £5.50 concession, £16 family.*

A mile southwest of town, off the A75 or reached by the lochside road, is this estate, the NTS horticultural school's magnificent floral extravaganza. The best time to visit is early spring when over 200 types of daffodils burst into bloom, but it's a very colourful experience at any time of the year. Now open to the public, the house can be viewed by guided tour only. There's a very good self-service restaurant in the visitor centre, see Restaurants, page 76.

Threave Castle

ⓘ *T0131-6688800 (HS), 1 Apr-30 Sep daily 0930-1630, Oct 0930-1530, £4.50, £3.60 concession, £2.70 child.*

Two miles further west at Bridge of Dee, a country lane branches north (right) and leads for about a mile to the start of a footpath which takes you to the gaunt tower of Threave Castle, standing alone on an island in the middle of the River Dee. Threave was built in the 14th century by Archibald 'the grim', third Earl of Douglas, and head of the 'Black' Douglas line. The Douglases were one of Scotland's most powerful baronial families and the main line, the 'Black' Douglases, were descended from 'the Good' Sir James, trusted friend of Robert the Bruce. The outer wall of the castle was added in 1450 in an unsuccessful attempt to defend it against King James II, who was determined to break the power of the maverick Border family. The Covenanters reduced Threave to its present ruinous state in 1640, and little remains of the interior. It's a romantic ruin nevertheless, especially as you have to be ferried across to the island. It's a half-mile walk from the car park, then ring the bell for the custodian to take you across in a small rowing boat. There's a tearoom at the car park.

Gatehouse of Fleet

The quiet little town of Gatehouse of Fleet lies 10 miles west of Kirkcudbright, a mile or so north of the A75. It's an attractive place on the banks of the Water of Fleet, surrounded by forested hills. On the main street, opposite the TIC, is the **Mill on the Fleet Museum** ⓘ *T01557-814099, www.millonthefleet.co.uk, Easter-Oct daily 1000-1700, free,* housed in a restored 18th-century cotton mill complete with working waterwheel. The museum traces the history of the town's cotton industry which lasted from the mid-18th century until the early 19th century. There's also a bookshop and a pleasant café with riverside terrace.

There are several pleasant walks in the surrounding countryside, including to **Cardoness Castle** ⓘ *T01557-814427 (HS), Apr-Sep daily 0930-1730, Oct-Mar Sat and Sun 0930-1630, £4, £3.20 concession, £2.40 child, about 1½ miles to the south, standing on a hill overlooking the B796 which connects Gatehouse with the main A75.* The remarkably well-preserved ruin was the home of the MacCullochs and is a classic example of a 15th-century tower house. There are excellent views across Fleet Bay from the top floor. Details of other local walks are given in a leaflet which is on sale at the tourist office. **Gatehouse of Fleet TIC** ⓘ *in the car park on the High St, T01557-814212, Mar, Apr and Oct daily 1000-1630, Jun and Sep till 1700, Jul and Aug till 1800.*

Between the Solway Firth and the Ayrshire coast lies Galloway Forest Park, the largest forest park in Britain, covering 300 square miles of forested hills, wild and rugged moorland and numerous lochs. It's a vast and beautiful area crisscrossed by waymarked Forestry Commission trails and longer routes, such as the Southern Upland Way, see page 71. It's home to a rich variety of fauna, such as feral goats, red deer, falcons and even golden eagles. It was also the first national park in the United Kingdom to be awarded Dark Sky Park status in November 2009 (see www.forestry.gov.uk/darkskygalloway) and is one of the best spots in the United Kingdom to stargaze with the naked eye.

Arriving in Galloway Forest Park
Getting there Newton Stewart is the main service town for Galloway Forest Park. It lies on the main A75 between Dumfries and Stranraer and there are regular buses to and from each of these destinations. ▶▶ *For further details, see Transport page 77.*

Getting around The best way to see the park is on foot or by bike. Those wishing to hike in the park should be properly equipped and buy the relevant Ordnance Survey maps. As well as the OS map, *The Galloway Hills: A Walker's Paradise*, by George Brittain, is also useful. National Cycle Route 7 incorporates 30 miles of off-road trails through the park, as well as the Raider's Road, see below.

Tourist information Newton Stewart TIC ① *Dashwood Sq, just off the main street and opposite the bus station, T01671-402431, Apr and Oct daily 1000-1630, May, Jun and Sep till 1700, Jul and Aug till 1800.* They can book accommodation for you (for a £3 fee) as well as provide lots of information on walking and cycling in Galloway Forest Park. See also their free guide to Ranger led walks and activities. There are visitor centres at Glentrool, Kirroughtree and Clatteringshaws (see below). The **Forestry Commission regional office** ① *T01671-402420, www.forestry.gov.uk/gallowayforestpark*, is at Creebridge, east of Newton Stewart. Glentrool and Kirroughtree are two of the famous 7stanes mountain-bike trails (www.7stanesmountainbiking.com).

The park → *Phone code: 01556. OS Outdoor Leisure Map No 32.*
The A712 runs northwest from Newton Stewart, cutting through the southern section of the Galloway Forest Park, to New Galloway. This 19-mile stretch of scenic road is known as **The Queen's Way**. Seven miles southwest of New Galloway the road skirts **Clatteringshaws Loch**, hidden amongst the pine trees, with a 14-mile footpath running round it. This path joins the Southern Upland Way which winds its way north towards the **Rhinns of Kells**, a range of hills around 2600 ft that form the park's eastern boundary. On the shores of the loch is the **Clatteringshaws Forest Wildlife Centre** ① *T01556-402420, Apr-Oct daily 1030-1700, free*, which gives an introduction to the park's flora and fauna. From the centre you can follow the lochside trail to **Bruce's Stone**, a huge boulder marking the spot where Robert the Bruce is said to have rested after yet another victory over those troublesome southern neighbours.

About a mile southwest of the centre, opposite the massive Clatteringshaws dam, is the turning for the **Raiders' Road**, a 10-mile timber road and erstwhile cattle rustlers' route which runs from the A712 and follows the Water of Dee southeast to Stroan Loch and then turns north to meet the A762 just north of Mossdale. About halfway along the trail is the otter's pool, in a clearing in the forest, a great place for a picnic. The Raider's Road is only open between April and October, and there's a toll charge. It can be driven but is best enjoyed on two wheels. The A762 heads north along the western shore of Loch Ken back to New Galloway, making a circuit of about 20 miles, starting and ending in New Galloway. About three miles southwest of Clatteringshaws Loch along The Queen's Way is the **Galloway Red Deer Range** ① *T07771-748401, www.forestry.gov.uk*, where you can get close up to the deer, stroke them and take photos. There are guided ranger walks from June to September but the highlight is 'Roaring Stags' in October. Check website for details.

About three miles east of Newton Stewart, near Palnure, is the **Kirroughtree Visitor Centre** ① *T01671-402165, Apr-Sep daily 1030-1700, Oct closes at 1630*, the southern gateway to Galloway Forest Park. A series of waymarked trails and cycle routes lead from here into the forest. There's also a tea room serving light meals. One of the most accessible and loveliest parts of Galloway Forest Park is **Glen Trool**. Ten miles north of Newton Stewart at Bargrennan, on the A714, a narrow road winds its way for five miles past Glen Trool Village to **Loch Trool**, hemmed in by the wooded slopes of the glen. Halfway up the loch is **Bruce's Stone**, which marks the spot where Robert the Bruce's guerrilla band ambushed the pursuing English force in 1307, after they had routed the main army at Solway Moss.

There are a number of excellent hiking trails which start out from here, including the one to the summit of **Merrick** (2766 ft), the highest peak in southern Scotland. It's a tough climb of about four hours, but fairly straightforward and well worth the effort. There are also numerous Forestry Commission trails for the less fit/experienced/ adventurous. Part of the **Southern Upland Way**, see page 71, runs through Glen Trool and along the southern shores of Loch Trool, then continues east towards Clatteringshaws Loch. On the road to Loch Trool, about a mile from the village, is the **Glen Trool Visitor Centre** ① *T01671-402420, Apr-Oct daily 1030-1730*.

New Galloway and around → *Phone code: 01644.*

One of the most convenient entry points for Galloway Forest Park is New Galloway, a pleasant little village of whitewashed houses nestled in the valley of **The Glenkens**, which runs north from Loch Ken. A few miles north of New Galloway is the village of **Dalry**, or St John's town of Dalry, to give it its full name, sitting beside the Water of Ken and giving access to the Southern Upland Way. About five miles farther north on the A713 is the turning to **Polmaddy Settlement**, a reconstructed Galloway village dating from before the Clearances of the 18th and 19th centuries.

Newton Stewart and around → *Phone code: 01671. Population: 3200.*

The amiable little town of Newton Stewart is a popular base for hiking in the hills of Galloway Forest Park, especially around **Glen Trool**. Set on the west bank of the River Cree at the junction of the main A75 and the A714, amidst beautiful wooded countryside, Newton Stewart is also a major centre for salmon and trout fishing. The season runs from March till mid-October. Permits, guides and the hire of fishing gear can all be arranged at the fishing tackle shops in town.

Four miles north of town, reached via the A714, is the **Wood of Cree Nature Reserve** ① *T01671-402861*, the largest ancient woodland in southern Scotland. This RSPB reserve is home to a huge variety of birdlife, including pied flycatchers, redstarts and wood warblers. There are nature trails running for two miles through the forest in the Cree

Valley. Southeast of town, just beyond Palnure, on the A75, is **Creetown**, standing on the east shore of Wigtown Bay, overlooked by the distinctive bulk of Cairnsmore of Fleet hill (2330 ft). Creetown is most notable for its **Gem Rock Museum** ① *T01671-820357, www. gemrock.net, Easter-Sep daily 0930-1730, Oct-Mar daily 1000-1600, £4, £3.50 concession, £2.50 child, £10.50 family*, which has a wide range of precious stones on display.

South of the A75 is the peninsula of fertile rolling farmland known as the Machars. It's a somewhat neglected corner of the southwest but has strong early Christian associations, and there are many important sites. The main town in the far southwest, Stranraer, wins no prizes for beauty or tourist appeal, but as Scotland's main ferry port for Northern Ireland it's an important town which sees a lot of through traffic. It sits on the shores of sheltered Loch Ryan on the Rhinns of Galloway, a windswept peninsula shaped like the head of a pick-axe at the end of the Solway Coast. Nine miles southwest of Stranraer on the windswept and rugged west coast of the Rhinns is the extremely photogenic old port of Portpatrick.

The Machars

The disconsolate little town of **Wigtown** sits on the northwesterly shore of Wigtown Bay and is notable for its large number of bookshops (18 at the last count). It is now gaining a reputation as Scotland's National Book Town with festivals held throughout the year, www.wigtown-booktown.co.uk. If you need to buy a book in the southwest, then this is the place to do it.

Eleven miles south from Wigtown is the village of **Whithorn**, which occupies a crucially place in Scotland's history. It was here in the fifth century, that **St Ninian** established a mission and built the first Christian church north of Hadrian's Wall. The tiny church, which he called **Candida Casa** (bright shining place), has not survived but after Ninian's death a priory was built to house his tomb. This became a famous seat of learning and an important place of pilgrimage for penitents from England and Ireland, as well as from Scotland. **Whithorn Story** ① *T01988-500508, Apr-Oct daily 1030-1700, £4.50, £3 concessions, £2.25 child, £12 family*, features artefacts uncovered by the archaeological dig in the ruins of the 12th-century priory and an audio-visual display telling the story of the area's development. The adjacent **Priory Museum** contains some important interesting archaeological finds and early Christian sculpture, including the Latinus Stone which dates from AD 450 and is the earliest Christian memorial in Scotland.

Four miles away is the misnamed **Isle of Whithorn**, which isn't an island at all but an atmospheric old fishing village built around a natural harbour. The village is the site of the ruined 13th-century **St Ninian's Chapel**, built for pilgrims who landed here from England and Ireland. Along the coast to the west of the village is **St Ninian's Cave**, said to have been used by the saint as a private place of prayer. It is reached via a footpath off the A747 before entering the Isle of Whithorn.

From Whithorn the A747 heads west to meet the coast and then runs northwest along the east shore of **Luce Bay** for 15 miles till it meets the A75 at the pretty little village of Glenluce. Two miles north of the village, signposted off the A75, is **Glenluce Abbey** ① *Apr-end Sep daily 0930-1730, £4, £3.20 concession, £2.40 child*, founded in 1192 by Roland, Earl of Galloway for the Cistercian order. The remains, set in a beautiful and peaceful valley, include a handsome early 16th-century Chapter House with a vaulted ceiling noted for its excellent acoustics. The abbey was visited by Robert the Bruce, James IV and, you guessed it, Mary, Queen of Scots. Buses 430 and 500 between Newton Stewart and Stranraer stop in Glenluce village and you can walk from there.

Stranraer

The main attraction here is the medieval tower which is all that remains of the 16th-century **Castle of St John** *T01776-705544, Jun-end Sep Tue-Sat 1000-1300 and 1330-1630, free*, one of the main headquarters of Graham of Claverhouse, the fanatical persecutor of the Protestant Covenanters in the late 17th century. Many of them died in the castle dungeons. It was later used as a prison in the 19th century. Inside, an exhibition traces the castle's history. Also worth a peek is the **Stranraer Museum** ⓘ *T01776-705088, all year Mon-Fri 1000-1700, Sat 1000-1300, 1330-1600, free*, which features displays on local history and has a section devoted to the life of Arctic explorer Sir John Ross (1777-1856), whose expeditions to find the Northwest Passage to the Pacific led to the discovery, in 1831, of the North Magnetic Pole. His house, called North West Castle, is now a hotel (see below). The **tourist information centre** ⓘ *28 Harbour St, T01776702595, Apr-Jun, Oct and Nov Mon-Sat 0930-1730, Sun 1000-1600, Jul-Sep Mon-Sat 0930-1730, Sun 1000-1630, Dec-Mar Mon-Sat 1000-1600.*

Three miles east of Stranraer are **Castle Kennedy Gardens** ⓘ *www.castlekennedy gardens.co.uk, Apr-Sep daily 1000-1700*, famous for their riotous rhododendrons and magnificent monkey puzzle trees. The 75 acres of landscaped gardens are set on a peninsula between two lochs and two castles – Castle Kennedy and Lochinch Castle. Check their website for various seasonal events throughout the year.

Portpatrick to the Mull of Galloway
Until the mid-19th century Portpatrick was the main departure point for Northern Ireland but is now a peaceful little holiday resort and a good base from which to explore the southern part of the peninsula. You can arrange sea fishing trips from here (£8 for half a day, T01776-810468). Portpatrick is also the starting point for the **Southern Upland Way**, the 212-mile coast-to-coast route which ends at Cockburnspath on the Berwickshire Coast, see below.

From Portpatrick the road runs south to the Mull of Galloway through lush, green farmland which receives high average rainfall. The Rhinns are also warmed by the Gulf Stream which gives the peninsula the mildest climate in Scotland and means it's almost frost-free. This is beautifully demonstrated at **Logan Botanic Garden** ⓘ *T01776-860231, www.rbge.org.uk, Mar-end Oct daily 1000-1700, Sun only in Feb, £5.50, £4.50 concession, £1 children, £11 family*, an outpost of Edinburgh's Royal Botanic Garden, about a mile north of the tiny village of Port Logan. The garden boasts a vast array of exotic, subtropical flora from the southern hemisphere, including tree ferns and cabbage palms. Bus No 407 from Stranraer passes through Port Logan on its way to Drummore.

Five miles further south is the **Mull of Galloway**, a dramatic, storm-lashed headland and Scotland's most southerly point, only 25 miles from Ireland and the Isle of Man. The narrow isthmus is an **RSPB nature reserve** and the home of thousands of seabirds such as guillemots, razorbills and puffins. There's a small **information centre** ⓘ *T01671-402861, late-May to Aug.*

Southern Upland Way
The most famous and demanding of walks, the 212-mile Southern Upland Way, running from Portpatrick to Cockburnspath on the Berwickshire Coast in the east, passes through a great variety of scenery from the Rhinns of Galloway to the wild heartland of Southern Scotland to the gentler eastern Borders. The most picturesque sections are the beginning and the end, but in between the highlights include Glen Trool, the Lowther Hills, St Mary's Loch and the River Tweed. A route leaflet is available from the **Countryside Ranger Service** ⓘ *Scottish Borders Council, Harestanes Visitor Centre, Ancrum, Jedburgh TD8 6UQ, T01835-830281.* There is also a trail pack available from the Dumfries and Galloway or Scottish Borders tourist boards. See also www.dumgal.gov.uk/southernuplandway.

Dumfries and Galloway listings

For hotel and restaurant price codes and other relevant information, see pages 12-19.

🛏 Where to stay

Annandale, Eskdale and the Lowther Hills *p55*

There's plenty of accommodation in Moffat but it's a busy place in Jul and Aug and you'll have to book ahead.

£££ Best Western Moffat House Hotel, Moffat, T01683-220039, www.moffathouse. co.uk. 20 rooms. This impressive mansion is the best of several hotels lining the High St. Has a good restaurant, the **Adam Library** (**£££-££**).

£££ Skirling House, at Skirling, about 3 miles northeast of Biggar, T01899-860274, www.skirlinghouse.com. Open Mar-Dec. This is a wonderful and tasteful B&B with superb home cooking (**£££**).

£££ Well View Private Hotel, Ballplay Rd, Moffat, T01683-220184. Overlooking the town is this lovely Victorian house with an excellent restaurant, see Restaurants, page 75.

£££-££ Famous Star Hotel, 44 High St, Moffat, T01683-220156, www.famous starhotel.com. Claims to be the narrowest hotel in the UK, so not for the large of waist.

£££-££ Hartfell House, Hartfell Cres, Moffat, T01683-220153, www.hartfellhouse. co.uk. Elegant and supremely comfortable guest house which is about a 10-min walk from the High St. Guests can also eat in their highly rated and very popular **Lime Tree Restaurant**.

££ Lindsaylands Country House B&B, 1 mile west of Biggar, T01899-220033. An excellent B&B.

£ Lotus Lodge, Wanlockhead, T01659-74252. Open Apr-Oct, on the Southern Upland Way, is this youth hostel.

Camping

Ewes Water Caravan & Camping Park, T01387-380386. Open Apr-Sep. Close to Langholm.

Hammerlands Farm, T01683-220436. Open Mar-Nov. About a mile east of Moffat by the A708, has a campsite.

Dumfries and around *p59, map p59*

££££ Comlongon Castle, T01387-870283, www.comlongon.co.uk. For a bit of luxury, try this 14th-century, family-owned castle and adjacent mansion house hotel. To get there, head north from Ruthwell for about a mile to Clarencefield, where a signposted road turns left (west) for another mile to the castle.

£££ Buccleuch and Queensberry Hotel, 112 Drumlanrig St, Thornhill, T01848-330215, www.buccleuchhotel.co.uk. 19th century coaching inn in the centre of the village. Very good restaurant.

£££ Cairndale Hotel, English St, Dumfries, T01387-254111, www.cairndalehotel.co.uk. 91 rooms. Popular with business visitors with excellent leisure facilities as well as a good restaurant, hosts a ceilidh on Sun nights (May-Oct). Check website for offers on weekend breaks.

£££ Cavens Country House Hotel, Kirkbean near New Abbey, T01387-880234, www.caverns.com. Country house hotel, once owned by tobacco baron, Robert Oswald. The perfect place to get away from whatever it is you want to get away from, and superb food at the **Steamboat Inn**, see page 75.

£££ Trigony House Hotel, Closeburn, Thornhill, 01843-331211, www.trigony hotel. co.uk. Former shooting lodge for Closeburn Castle, Trigony combines the traditional estate living with the cosy hospitality of a family home. Ideal base for fishing and walking holiday but it is the food that really sets it apart. Everything is home-made, using organic produce from their

own garden and the best in local game and fish. Highly recommended.
££ Cairngill House Hotel, Kippford, T01387-780681. Comfortable

There are many B&B options in Dumfries in the **££-£** price range. Ask at the tourist office. Those listed below offer good value and comfort.
££-£ Fulwood Hotel, 30 Lovers Walk, Dumfries, T01387-252262. Close to the train station.
££-£ Hazeldean House, 4 Moffat Rd, Dumfries, T01387-266178, www.hazeldeanhouse.com. 6 en suite rooms. Private parking.
££-£ The Merlin, 2 Kenmure Terr, Dumfries, T01387-261002. Nicely located overlooking the river near the Burns Centre.
££-£ Morton Villa, 28 Lovers Walk, Dumfries, T01387-255825. Lovely Victorian house opposite the train station. Caters for vegetarians.
Self-catering accommodation is plentiful in Rockliffe. Contact the tourist board for further details, see page 60. **National Trust for Scotland** have a lovely cottage right on the beach, sleeps 5, £250-550 per week, see page 15 for details.
Craigbittern House, at Sandyhills, about a mile east of Colvend, T01387-780247, www.craigbitterncottage.co.uk. Another excellent option.

Camping
There are some good campsites in the Rockliffe/Kippford area.
Castle Point Caravan Site, T01556-630248. Open Mar-Oct. Near Rockliffe.
Kippford Holiday Park, T01556-620636, www.kippfordholidaypark.co.uk.
Sandyhills Bay Leisure Park, T01387-780257. Open Apr-Oct. Pick of the bunch is this wonderfully sited option.

Kirkcudbright, Castle Douglas and around *p64*
££££-£££ Balcary House Hotel, Auchencairn, T01556-640217, www.balcary-bay-hotel. co.uk. Open Mar-Oct. 20 rooms. Luxurious, family-run country house hotel set in 3 acres of garden, overlooking lovely Auchencairn Bay. Excellent restaurant, see page 75.
££££-£££ Cally Palace Hotel & Golf Course, Gatehouse of Fleet, T0844-4889695, www.mcmillanhotels.co.uk. Set in 500 acres of its own grounds, this very exclusive Georgian mansion and former home of local laird James Murray who amassed a massive fortune from the cotton industry, offers impeccable luxury and top-class facilities, including private 18-hole golf course and indoor pool.
£££-££ Craigadam, 11 miles out Castle Douglas, on the A712 near Crockettford, T01556-650233, www.craigadam.com. 6 en suite rooms. Elegant country house and working farm where you can enjoy good home cooking (**£££** with evening meal).
£££-££ Selkirk Arms Hotel, High St, Kirkcudbright, T01557-330402, www.selkirkarmshotel. co.uk. 17 rooms. The top hotel in town. Beautifully refurbished Georgian building with attractive rooms and also has the town's finest restaurant, see Restaurants, page 75.
££ Albion House, 49 Ernespie Rd, Castle Douglas, T01556-502360, www.albionhousecastledouglas.co.uk. Best of the B&Bs in town.
££ Baytree House, 110 High St, Kirkcudbright, T01557-330824, www.baytreekirkcudbright.co.uk. 4 en suite rooms. Georgian house with nice touches throughout. Good food available. No smoking. Great value.
££ Gladstone House, 48 High St, Kirkcudbright, T01557-331734, kirkcudbrightgladstone.com. 3 en suite rooms. This wonderful, superior guest house has a secluded garden and also offers dinner

(**£££-££**). No smoking. A cracking place to stay, fantastic value.

££ The Greengate, 46 High St, Kirkcudbright, T01557-331895, www.thegreengate.co.uk. 1 en suite room. Former home of artists Jessie M King and E A Taylor. No smoking.

Camping

Loch Ken Holiday Park, by the village of Parton, T01644-470282, www.lochkenhol idaypark.freeserve.co.uk. Open late-Mar to early Nov (see also What to do, below).

Lochside Caravan & Camping Site, beside the loch, Castle Douglas, T01557-503806. Open Easter-late Oct.

Seaward Caravan Park, Kirkcudbright, T01557-870267. Open Mar-Oct. Part of a new leisure complex at Brighouse Bay, with a wide range of facilities including heated pool, 9-hole golf course and pony trekking.

Silvercraigs Caravan & Camping Site, T01557-503806. Open Easter to late-Oct. On an elevated site overlooking the Kirkcudbright, about a 10-min walk from the centre.

Galloway Forest Park *p67*

££££ Kirroughtree House, Newton Stewart, T844-488 9695, www.macmillan hotels.co.uk. 17 rooms. Another of McMillan Hotels' southwest stable of grand hotels, this grand 18th-century country mansion is set in its own grounds and offers impeccable standards of comfort and service. Its superb restaurant has a well-deserved reputation for its gourmet Scottish cuisine.

£££ Creebridge House Hotel, across the river in the village of Minnigaff, near Newton Stewart, T01671-402121, www.creebridge. co.uk. 19 rooms. Nice location, good food in restaurant or bistro.

££ Stables Guest House, Corsbie Rd, Newton Stewart, T01671-402157, www.stablesguesthouse.com. 6 rooms. Comfortable. Very good value. No smoking.

£ SYHA Youth Hostel, Newton Stewart, T01671-402211. Open mid-Mar to end Oct, in the village of Minnigaff, which is on the other side of the river, across the bridge.

£ Youth Hostel, Kendoon, T01644-460680, 5 miles north of Dalry on the B7000, close to the Southern Upland Way and the A713. Open mid-Mar to early Oct. Take the Castle Douglas-Ayr bus and ask to get off near the hostel.

Camping

Glen Trool Holiday Park, T01671-840280. Open Mar-Oct. Near Glen Trool village, just off the A714.

The far southwest *p70*

££££ Corsewall Lighthouse Hotel, 11 miles northwest of Stranraer at Corsewall Point, T01776-853220,www.lighthouse hotel.co.uk. 11 suites and rooms. This cosy hotel is housed in a working lighthouse, set in 20 acres of its own grounds on the wild and windy clifftops, and is a surreal experience. The owners can arrange transport from Stranraer.

££££ Knockinaam Lodge Hotel, Portpatrick, T01776-810471, www. knockinaamlodge.com. By far the best place to stay in this area, a wonderful place which offers great sea views, exquisite and unmatched cuisine, see Restaurants, page 76, and impeccable service. It is rated as one of the best hotels in the south of Scotland.

£££ Fernhill Hotel, Stranraer, T0844-488 9695, www.mcmillanhotels.co.uk. Those without the means to enjoy the splendours of **Knockinaam Lodge** can try this McMillan hotel which overlooks the village. Its restaurant has a fine reputation.

£££ North West Castle Hotel, Stranraer. 73 rooms. This is yet another McMillan Hotel and the most luxurious choice in the area. The former home of Sir John Ross (see page 70) also offers full leisure facilities and excellent cuisine.

££ Steam Packet Inn, Isle of Whithorn, T01988-500354, www.steampacketinn.biz. A popular fishermen's pub with rooms on the quayside, which serves good, cheap bar meals.

Restaurants

Annandale, Eskdale and the Lowther Hills p55

£££ Well View Private Hotel, see Where to stay, page 72. Locally renowned for its excellent use of the best of local produce. 6-course dinner is lavish and expensive, lunch is mid-range and served Sun-Thu.

££ Claudio's Restaurant, in the old police station at Burnside, Moffat, T01683-220958, www.claudiosmoffat.co.uk. Sun-Thu till 2130, Fri/Sat till 2200, Sep-May closed Mon. Serves a range of Italian dishes.

££ The Lime Tree, part of the Hartfell House guesthouse (see under Where to stay, page 72).

££ Riverside Inn, Canonbie, near Langholm, T01387-371512. Serves superb pub food.

Dumfries and around p59, map p59

££ Anchor Hotel, Kippford, T01556-620205, www.anchorhotelkippford.co.uk. Serves superb pub food and is the perfect spot for a great pint of real ale after the walk from Rockcliffe.

££ Auld Alliance Restaurant, 60 Moffat Rd, Dumfries, T01387-256800, www.theauld alliancedumfries.co.uk. As the name suggests, it's a mixture of Scottish and French culinary styles, and features delights such as local queen scallops in garlic butter with smoked Ayrshire bacon and Galloway cream, also whisky, honey and oatmeal ice cream.

££ Criffel Inn, New Abbey, T01387-850244, www.criffel-inn.co.uk. Food daily 1200-1400 and 1700-2000. Great village pub serving good bar meals. Beer garden and good selection of ales.

££ Hector's Kitchen, 20a Academy St, Dumfries, T01387-256263. Mon-Sat 0900-1500 and 1730-2130. International menu featuring such diverse temptations as Tempura vegetable salad and pan-crusted sea bass, also tex-mex and pasta. Cheap lunches. Shiny, happy decor matched by the friendliness of the owners. No smoking.

££ Hullabaloo, Mill Rd, Dumfries, T01387-259679, above the Burns Centre in a converted old water mill. Mon 1100-1600, Tue-Sat 1100-1600 and 1800-2200, Sun 1100-1500. Chilled atmos by day with good selection of wraps, baguettes and bagels, by night menu features pastas, steaks and salads plus daily specials and decent wine list. Beer garden for those rare summer rays.

££ Opus Salad Bar, 95 Queensbury St, Dumfries, T01387-255752. Mon-Sat 0900-1630, Thu till 1415. One of the few vegetarian eateries.

££ Steamboat Inn, Carsethorn, near New Abbey, T01387-880631, www.steamboatinn carsethorn.co.uk. Food daily 1200-1430, 1830-2300. Location alone would be enough for the **Steamboat** to be included, sitting at the end of a dead-end road looking across the Solway Firth, but blow me if they don't go and serve some of the best pub grub this side of Hadrian's Wall. On top of all that, they have a good selection of beers and malts.

Kirkcudbright, Castle Douglas and around p64

£££ Balcary House Hotel, Auchencairn, see Where to stay, page 73. Mon-Sat dinner by arrangement, Sun 1200-1400. Enjoy the modern Scottish dinner menu or Sunday lunch in the conservatory. Either way, this is a rare treat.

£££ Selkirk Arms Hotel, see Where to stay, page 73. Food served daily 1200-1400 and 1800-2130. The best place to eat in Kirkcudbright, the highly skilled chef is something of a local celebrity. Restaurant specializes in local fish and seafood while the bistro offers a more affordable alternative.

££ Carlo's, 211 King St, Castle Douglas, T01556-503977, www.carlosrestaurant. co.uk. Open for dinner only. Italian restaurant offering the only real alternative to the town's hotel dining rooms or bars.

££ Crown Hotel, 25-26 King S, Castle Douglas, T01556-502031, www.thecrown hotelcd.co.uk. Probably the best option for a bar meal in town. Lunch is particularly good value.

££ Murray Arms Hotel, Gatehouse of Fleet, T01557-814207, www.murrayarmshotel. co.uk. Food served 1200-1400, 1700-2130. Extensive dinner menu featuring local beef, fish and seafood, lunch a little less adventurous but cheaper.

££-£ Gordon House Hotel, 116 High St, Kirkcudbright, T01557-330670, www. gordon-house-hotel.co.uk. Food served 1200-1400, 1800-2100. **Marshall's Restaurant** offers a decent Modern Scottish menu while the bar meals served next door are very good value.

£ Designs Café, 179 King St, Castle Douglas, T01556-504552. Healthy lunch specials served Mon-Sat 1200-1500. Downstairs, at rear of gallery and shop, very relaxed, attentive service and good.

£ Purdie's Delicatessen & Sandwich Bar, 173 King St, Castle Douglas. Mon-Sat 0830-1600. Best sandwiches in town (to take away).

£ Riverside Café, High St, Gatehouse of Fleet, Mill on the Fleet, T01557-814977, www.millonthefleet.co.uk. Daily 1000-1700. Salads and other typical lunchtime dishes, good value.

£ The Terrace, Threave Garden and Estate, see page 66. Self-service restaurant in NTS Visitor Centre using the finest produce from their own garden. Great spot for lunch but food served all day during opening hours.

Galloway Forest Park *p67*
£££ Kirroughtree House, Newton Stewart, see Where to stay, page 74. The best place to eat for miles. Worth the expense.

££-£ Black Sheep Inn, T01671-404326, about half a mile out of Newton Stewart on the A714 heading south is this licensed restaurant and bar.

The far southwest *p70*
As well as these options, you can try hotel bar meals or the numerous fast food outlets.

£££ Knockinaam Lodge, see Where to stay, page 74. The best place to eat in Portpatrick and one of the very best in the south of Scotland.

£££ North West Castle Hotel, Stranraer, see Where to stay, page 74. The most expensive place to eat in the area.

££ Waterfront Hotel and Bistro, seafront, Portpatrick, T01776-810800. Good value lunch and dinner featuring local seafood.

££ L'Aperitif, London Rd, Stranraer, T01776-702991. Mon-Sat 1200-1400 and 1730-2100. Serves good Italian food.

Bars and clubs

Dumfries and around *p59, map p59*
Globe Inn, 56 High St, Dumfries. Atmospheric old place, famous as the favourite watering hole of a certain poet of this parish. **The Mint** (formerly **Caffe Bar Identity**), 23 Bank St, Dumfries. Open till 0100 at weekends. Type of trendy bar that will probably have changed hands by the time you read this. Big-screen sports and bar menu.

Entertainment

Dumfries and around *p59, map p59*
RBC Film theatre, Burns Centre, Dumfries, T01387-264808. Good programme of arthouse and mainstream cinema.

Festivals

Annandale, Eskdale and the Lowther Hills *p55*
In Langholm, local festivals include the town's **Common Riding**, which takes place on the last weekend in **Jul**, the **Langholm & Eskdale Festival of Music and Arts** which is held in the last week in **Aug**, and the **Eskdale Agricultural Show** held at the end of **Sep**.

Amongst the local festivals held in Moffat is the **Moffat Agricultural Show**, held on the last Sat in **Aug**.

In the Lowther Hills, the **Scottish and British Gold Panning Championships** are held in Wanlockhead during the 2nd last weekend in **May**.

Dumfries and around p59, map p59
Dumfries Book Fair at the beginning of **May**, and **Guid Nychburris Festival** in the middle of **Jun**, which features a week of entertainment and ceremonies. On the 2nd Sat in **Aug** is the **Dumfries & Lockerbie Agricultural Show**. For a full list of dates, check with the tourist office. On the first Sat in **Aug** Palnackie hosts the **World Flounder Tramping Championships**, an unusual event which involves trying to catch the biggest flounder – with your feet!

Kirkcudbright, Castle Douglas and around p64
In Kirkcudbright, the **Kirkcudbright Arts Festival**, takes place over 2 weeks in late **Aug** and early **Sep** in venues throughout the town. **Kirkcudbright Jazz Festival** is held in mid **Jun**. Check out www.summerfestivities.com.

Castle Douglas now hosts the **Scottish Alternative Games** on the first Sun in **Aug**. The various traditional Scottish games include the world finals of the Gird'n'Cleek competition, spinnin' the peerie and snail racing. More details at www.lochkenholidaypark.freeserve.co.uk.

☯ What to do

Kirkcudbright, Castle Douglas and around p64
Galloway Sailing Centre, Parton, T01644-420626, www.lochken.co.uk. Apr-Oct daily 0900-1900, Nov-Mar daily till 1700. Offers tuition and hire for windsurfers, canoes and dinghies, as well as other activities such as quad biking and gorge scrambling. Also hot showers, hot and cold snacks and basic dormitory accommodation (**£**).
GM Marine Services, Kirkcudbright, T01557-331557. Contact TIC for times. £5, concession/

child £2.50. Run wildlife cruises up and down the River Dee on the Lovely Nellie. Leave from the marina (behind Broughton House).
Loch Ken Marina, near the village of Parton. Easter-31 Oct daily 0900-1700. Hires boats, canoes, bikes and issues fishing permits.
Longsheds Equestrian, Kelton, 2 miles from Castle Douglas, past Threave Garden, T01556-680498. For horse riding.

⊖ Transport

Annandale, Eskdale and the Lowther Hills p55
To **Gretna** and **Ecclefechan**, there are buses from Dumfries. Gretna Green is also on the Dumfries-Carlisle rail line and there are regular trains in either direction. Ecclefechan is served by buses that run between Lockerbie and Annan.

Langholm is on the No 95 bus route between Carlisle and Galashiels, and buses pass through several times daily. Bus No 124 (Yellow Bus) runs between Langholm and Eskdalemuir, and No 112 (MacEwans) runs betwenn Eskdalemuir and Lockerbie.

From **Moffat**, there are frequent buses to Edinburgh, Glasgow (No X74) and Dumfries (Nos 114 and 199). Bus No 199 also runs to Edinburgh, via the A708, on Fri and Sat. Bus No 382 runs to Carlisle, via Lockerbie and Gretna Green, and bus No 130 runs to Galashiels, via Selkirk, along the scenic A708. The main operator is **Stagecoach Western Buses**, T01387-253496. There's also the **Harrier Scenic Bus Service**, which runs once or twice a week between Jul and Sep – useful for walkers (see also page 29). For **Harrier Service** bus times call **First Edinburgh**, T0131-6639233.

From **Biggar** there are several daily buses to Edinburgh. There are also regular daily buses to Lanark. A **postbus** service, T01752-494527, runs to Tweedsmuir, Abington and Wanlockhead.

For the **Lowther Hills** there's a bus (No 223) to Leadhills from Sanquhar which passes through Wanlockhead.

Dumfries and around *p59, map p59*
From **Dumfries** there are regular buses
to **Kirkcudbright** (Nos 76, 501, X74).
No 500 and X75 go twice daily to **Newton
Stewart** (1 hr 20 mins) and **Stranraer**
(2 hrs), for the ferry to **Belfast**. National
Express, T08705-808080, runs a daily service
between **London** and **Belfast**, via **Dumfries**
and **Stranraer** and towns in between.
Stagecoach Western, T01292-613500,
has 2 buses daily to and from **Edinburgh**
(No 100; 2 hrs 20 mins). There are also
regular buses to **Carlisle** (No 79; 50 mins)
and to **Moffat** (No 114 or X74; 1 hr). Bus
No 500 runs to **Castle Douglas** (45 mins)
and No 246 to **Cumnock**, via **Sanquhar**
(50 mins). There are also buses to **Thornhill**,
Dalbeattie via **Rockcliffe**, **Moniaive**,
Glencaple/ Caerlaverock Castle and
Annan via **Ruthwell**. Bus No 372 runs from
Dumfries to **Dalbeattie**, stopping in **New
Abbey**, **Kirkbean**, **Rockcliffe** and **Kippford**,
T710357. There are frequent trains Mon-Sat
to and from **Carlisle** (35 mins) and several
daily (Mon-Sat) to and from **Glasgow**
(1½ hrs), via **Kilmarnock**, where you change
for trains to **Stranraer**. There's a reduced
service on Sun.

    Car hire from **Arnold Clark**, New Abbey
Rd, Dumfries, T01387-247151. Open Mon-Fri
0800-1800, Sat 0830-1700, Sun 1100-1700.

    Cycle hire from **Nithsdale Cycle Centre**,
46 Brooms Rd, Dumfries, T01387-254870.
Daily 1000-1700. For bike repairs and parts
go to **Kirkpatrick Cycles**, 13-15 Queen St,
Dumfries, T01387-254011. In Mabie Forest
is **Riks Bike Shed**, T01387-270275, open
Mon-Sat 1000-1800, Sun 1000-1600, see
page 61, for hire and trips out. Also has a
shop at Drumlanrig Castle (see page 62).

Kirkcudbright, Castle Douglas and around *p64*
Bus No 500 travels between **Dumfries** and
Stranraer stopping in **Gatehouse of Fleet**.
No 500 and X75 run between Gatehouse
of Fleet and **Newton Stewart**. McEwan's
bus Nos 501 and 505 run frequently from

Dumfries to **Kirkcudbright**, stopping in
Castle Douglas. Bus No 520 runs north
along the east shore of **Loch Ken** from
Castle Douglas to **New Galloway** and **Dalry**.

    Cycle hire from W Law, 19 St Cuthbert St,
Kirkcudbright, T01557-330579, and **Castle
Douglas Cycle Centre**, 11 Church St, Castle
Douglas, T01556-504542. Mon-Wed, Fri, Sat
0900-1230, 1330-1700.

Galloway Forest Park *p67*
Buses X75 and 500 run between **Dumfries**
and **Stranraer**, stopping in **Newton Stewart**
and other towns en route. There's also a
No 430 bus to Stranraer. **Newton Stewart**
is the departure point for buses south to
Wigtown and **Whithorn** (No 415). There's
a service (No 359) north along the A714
to **Girvan**, via Bargrennan and **Glen Trool**
village several times a day Mon-Sat (less
frequently on Sun). Yellow Bus S2, **Castle
Douglas** to **Dalry**, stops in **New Galloway**.
Some of these buses continue to **Ayr**. There
are also regular buses to **Dumfries**, Nos 503
and 501.

The far southwest *p70*
In **Stranraer**, the main transport hub,
transport links are all conveniently located
close to each other. The train station is on
the ferry pier, close to the **Stena Line** ferry
terminal, www.stenaline.co.uk, from where
car and passenger ferries leave for Belfast.
A few mins' walk south is the bus station.

    P&O ferries to Larne, www.poferries.com,
leave from **Cairnryan**, 5 miles north of
Stranraer on the A77. Bus No 358 and
X58 runs to Cairnryan from Stranraer.
For details on services to Northern Ireland,
see page 55.

    National Express, www.nationalexpress.
com, No 920 runs between **London** and
Belfast via **Stranraer** at 0945 and overnight.
Ulster Bus has services between **Belfast** and
Glasgow/Edinburgh via **Stranraer**. Booking
is essential on all these services. Stagecoach
Western has a service from **Glasgow** (3 hrs)
to Ayr (X77), change at **Ayr** for Stranraer.

There are regular buses to **Newton Stewart**, **Kirkcudbright**, **Dumfries** and other towns along the A75. There are also regular daily buses to Ayr (2 hrs), and daily buses to **Portpatrick** (25 mins), **Port Logan** (35 mins) and **Drummore** (45 mins).

There are several trains daily to **Belfast** via **Larne**. There's also a daily service to and from **Glasgow** (2 hrs) and Ayr (1 hr 20 mins). For all rail enquiries call T08457-484950.

● Directory

Dumfries and around *p59, map p59*
Banks All the major banks have branches with ATMs in the centre.

Kirkcudbright, Castle Douglas and around *p64*
Library, King St, Castle Douglas, T01557-502643. Free access. Mon-Wed and Fri 1000-1930, Thu and Sat 1000-1700.

Contents

Footnotes

Glossary

auld	old	glaikit	gormless
aye	yes	girn	moan/whinge
bairn	child	greet	cry
ben	hill or mountain	haar	sea mist
besom	cheeky/rascal	hen	dear (female person)
blether	to talk nonsense	howff	traditional pub/haunt
bonny	pretty	keek	look furtively
bothy	farm cottage/mountain hut	ken	know
brae	hill or slope	kirk	church
braw	beautiful	lade	mill stream
breeks	trousers	laird	landowner/squire
brig	bridge	lassie	girl
burn	brook	links	coastal golf course
canny	careful	lug	ear
ceilidh	social gathering involving singing, dancing and drinking	lum	chimney
		Mac/Mc	prefix in Scottish surnames denoting 'son of'
clan	tribe bearing same surname	machair	sandy, grassy coastal land used for grazing
Clearances	evictions of tenant crofters by landowners in the Highlands in late 18th and early 19th centuries in order to create space for more profitable sheep	manse	vicarage
		merse	saltmarsh
		mind	remember
		muckle	big
		munro	mountain over 3000 ft
close	narrow passage between buildings	neep	turnip
		nicht	night
clype	tell-tale	nippit	tight fitting
couthy	cosy	oxter	armpit
crannog	Celtic lake or bog dwelling	partan	large crab
croft	small plot of farmland and house	peely wally	pale/wan
		pend	alleyway
cuddie	horse	pinkie	little finger
doo	dove	poke	paper bag
dour	hard/stubborn	provost	mayor
dram	small measure of whisky	puddock	frog
drouthy	thirsty	reek	smoke
dunt	bump	sair	sore
elder	office bearer in Presbyterian church	Sassenach	literally 'southerner' though commonly used to describe English
factor	manager of estate/landlord		
firth	estuary	scunner	nuisance/disgust
fash	trouble/bother	sept	branch of clan
gallus	cheeky/forward	shoogle	shake
ghillie	personal hunting or fishing guide	sleekit	sly/cunning
		smirr	fine rain

sort	fix/mend	**wee**	small
tattie bogle	scarecrow	**wee Frees**	Followers of the Free
thole	endure		Church of Scotland
trauchled	tired and bothered	**wynd**	lane
wabbit	exhausted	**yett**	gate or door
wean	child		

Index

Notes